GEORGE CRABBE

GEORGE CRABBE

Selected Poetry

Edited with an Introduction
and Notes by
JEM POSTER

Carcanet / MidNAG

First published in Great Britain 1986
by the Carcanet Press
208 Corn Exchange Buildings
Manchester M4 3BQ
and
Mid Northumberland Arts Group
Town Hall, Ashington
Northumberland NE63 8RX

British Library Cataloguing in Publication Data

Crabbe, George
  Selected Poetry
  I. Title
  821'.7   PR4511

ISBN 0-85635-621-2 (Carcanet)
ISBN 0-904790-50-9 (MidNAG)

The Publisher acknowledges financial assistance
from the Arts Council of Great Britain

Typeset by Bryan Williamson, Swinton, Berwickshire
Printed in Great Britain by SRP Ltd, Exeter

Contents

Introduction

EVEN in old age George Crabbe would walk out alone in the roughest weather to the quarries around his son's home, stopping to uproot specimens of the rarer plants he encountered on his way and returning laden with them and with fossils hacked from the blue lias: 'dirty fossils', notes his more fastidious son, perhaps not entirely happy about the poet's tendency to spread them around the bedroom. It is worth registering from the outset the enduring intimacy of Crabbe's contact with the world, the sheer physicality of his grasp of things: the strengths of the poetry are more easily understood if we can visualise him actually grubbing at the slimy roots of the marsh-plants he so vividly described, delivering a neighbour's child, or assisting his father by piling butter-casks in a quayside warehouse.

Crabbe's father was warehouse-keeper, later collector of salt-duties, for the Customs at Aldborough in Suffolk; himself a man of some intellectual ability, he encouraged his son's literary interests and ensured that he received an adequate if limited schooling before apprenticing him to an apothecary in the hope that he might eventually make his way in the world as a surgeon. In this he was disappointed: Crabbe made little progress with his medical studies, and late in 1779 decided finally to abandon them for the precarious life of a literary adventurer in London.

He had little enough to build on. In 1775 an Ipswich bookseller had printed his 'Inebriety', a satire composed in unashamed imitation of Pope, but this 'trifle', as Crabbe disarmingly and not inaccurately termed it, provided no entrée into the London literary world; he was, moreover, entirely without influential social connections and desperately short of money. In his quest for a publisher, and subsequently for a patron, he exposed himself to a series of rebuffs particularly painful to a man of his rather morbid sensitivity: the diaries

7

he kept during those early months in London show him contending not only with poverty but with a sense of rejection which had assumed disturbing spiritual overtones:

Why art thou so far from me, O my Lord? why hidest thou thy face? I am cast down, I am in poverty and in affliction: be thou with me, O my God; let me not be wholly forsaken, O my Redeemer!

It was Edmund Burke who finally responded to Crabbe's appeals for patronage, transforming his prospects with almost fairytale rapidity. Crabbe approached Burke early in 1781; by the end of that year he had seen the publication of his long descriptive poem 'The Library' hailed with muted cordiality by the critics, and been admitted to deacon's orders. In 1782 Burke's recommendation secured him the post of domestic chaplain to the Duke of Rutland, while the following year saw his poetic reputation handsomely consolidated by the publication of 'The Village' and his frustratingly long engagement to Sarah Elmy, the daughter of a Suffolk tanner, crowned by marriage.

According to his son, the poet was eminently well fitted for domestic life; but the early deaths of all but two of his children and the subsequent deterioration of his wife's health cheated him of much of the pleasure he might have derived from that source. Sarah's condition was one of mental as well as physical imbalance, and she was subject to violent alternations of mood, swinging helplessly between blank despair and an agitated and voluble gaiety; at times her fear of being left alone kept Crabbe a virtual prisoner in his own home. 'Nothing can be more sincere than this', he commented on one of her early letters, 'nothing more reasonable and affectionate; and yet happiness was denied.' That consciousness of blighted promise underlies much of the poetry of his later years.

It is to those later years that the bulk of Crabbe's work belongs. After 'The Newspaper', printed in 1785 and so markedly inferior to 'The Village' as to suggest in itself a hiatus in his poetic development, he published no poetry for over twenty-two years; it was not until the autumn of 1807 that he returned to his public with a collection which included, besides 'The Library', 'The Village' and 'The Newspaper', a number of new poems, of which the most substantial and significant was 'The Parish Register'. The volume was favourably received; and with the publication of *The Borough* in 1810 and the *Tales* in 1812, Crabbe firmly established for himself an eminent position in a literary world which, while registering the rugged unfashionableness of his verse, nevertheless paid generous tribute to its originality and power.

Crabbe's wife died in 1813, and in the summer of the following year the poet made the last of his numerous moves, accepting from the Duke of Rutland the living of Trowbridge in Wiltshire. Although he was to remark to Thomas Campbell in 1817 that he had scarcely known positive happiness since the death of his wife, these events clearly marked the beginning of a freer and brighter passage in his life: his health, indifferent for many years, improved noticeably; he began to address his attentions to his female acquaintances, embarking on a series of mildly flirtatious relationships which, if they came to nothing, seem nevertheless to have afforded him a degree of innocent satisfaction; and he began once again to move in the artistic and aristocratic circles from which his marriage had effectively removed him.

After the publication of the *Tales*, Crabbe occupied himself with the preparation of a further volume, *Tales of the Hall*, which appeared in 1819; the sale of the copyright of this volume, together with that of his earlier works, fetched him the then considerable sum of £3,000. Although no more of his poetry was published in his lifetime, he continued to compose and revise until shortly before his death at Trowbridge in 1832: the understandably patchy results of his labours, the *Posthumous Tales*, were brought out under the auspices of his son in the *Life and Poems* of 1834.

*

It was Crabbe's explicit hope that the readers of his poems would 'feel them true', and the burden of his contemporaries' criticism that they did so. Byron, who considered Crabbe, in partnership with Coleridge, as 'the first of these times, in point of power and genius', set him up against the purveyors of 'splendid lies':

> ...Truth sometimes will lend her noblest fires,
> And decorate the verse herself inspires:
> This fact in Virtue's name let Crabbe attest;
> Though nature's sternest painter, yet the best.

Francis Jeffrey's influential championship of Crabbe in the pages of the *Edinburgh Review* also tended to focus on 'the exquisite truth of his delineations'; while even Wordsworth, who in 1808 had dismissed the bulk of Crabbe's poetry to date as too narrowly preoccupied with 'mere matters of fact', asserted in later life that his works would 'last, from their combined merits as Poetry and Truth, full as long as any thing that has been expressed in verse since they first made their appearance'.

The vigour and determination of Crabbe's drive towards truth became apparent at an early stage in his poetic career: in 'The Village', he deliberately countered the idealised pastoral of Goldsmith's 'Deserted Village' with a series of detailed descriptions of the harsh realities of rural life as he himself knew it. Strength rather than subtlety is the keynote here, as Crabbe ruthlessly strips away the 'tinsel trappings of poetic pride'; yet even in this early work, in lines which qualify his more robust assertions or concede partial validity to an alternative viewpoint, he is reaching towards the altogether more subtle and complex vision of truth which informs the poems of his maturity.

He is clearly seeking to define that vision when, in Letter XXIV of *The Borough*, he discusses the role of the poet in terms which pointedly insist upon a view of his subject matter as variform, mutable, equivocal:

> ...the Poet looks the world around,
> Where form and life and reasoning man are found:
> He loves the mind, in all its modes, to trace,
> And all the manners of the changing race;
> Silent he walks the road of life along,
> And views the aims of its tumultuous throng:
> He finds what shapes the Proteus-passions take,
> And what strange waste of life and joy they make,
> And loves to show them in their varied ways,
> With honest blame or with unflattering praise:
> 'T is good to know, 't is pleasant to impart,
> These turns and movements of the human heart.

If the passage itself is depressingly lifeless, it is nevertheless a pointer to the sources of Crabbe's power; for the 'turns and movements' so clumsily dissected here constitute an organic and essential feature of those poems in which his peculiar genius asserts itself most forcefully. Character, he insists again and again, is not fixed but kaleidoscopically mobile, subject, as in 'The Parting Hour', to the depredations of time or, as in 'The Dumb Orators', responding to pressures exerted upon it by its social context; and of itself volatile, sometimes to the point of indeterminacy. The description of the old alms-house inhabitant, Blaney, in Letter XIV of *The Borough* brings into sharp focus the disconcerting ambivalence central to many of Crabbe's finest characterisations:

> Misery and mirth are blended in his face,
> Much innate vileness and some outward grace;
> There wishes strong and stronger griefs are seen,
> Looks ever changed, and never one serene.

Blaney's unrest has disturbing moral implications of which Crabbe was certainly acutely aware, but it is also a form of affirmation: it is not simply that such ambivalence imparts a powerful dramatic charge to the poetry but also, and doubtless

11

for Crabbe more importantly, that it bespeaks a richness and dynamism in humanity itself. The point is made clearly enough in the depiction of two characters in *The Borough* who are actually notable for their unperturbed evenness of spirit: the 'peaceful mind' of the vicar in Letter III is revealed in the course of Crabbe's probing analysis to be pathetically inert, while the equanimity of the 'prudent and temperate' benefactor described in Letter XVII is explicitly defined as inadequate:

'Is aught then wanted in a man so wise?' –
Alas! – I think he wants infirmities;
He wants the ties that knit us to our kind....

Crabbe's registering of the importance to humanity of the dialectic of the divided spirit is paralleled by suggestions of an equivalent need in interpersonal relationships. The fastidiousness of Nancy in 'The Widow's Tale' runs counter to the earthiness of both her family and her suitor, and initially separates her from them; but in a conclusion which plainly defines the opposing forces as mutually redemptive, Crabbe directs us towards an understanding of the positive energies implicit in such tensions. Similarly, he brings together in the characters of Sybil and Josiah in 'The Frank Courtship' a vitality which comes dangerously close to superficiality and a decency bordering on stuffiness, and then uses the thrust and counter-thrust of a deftly manipulated dialogue to show how valuably each may qualify the other. There is a further and highly significant opposition here, between the vibrant synthesis arrived at through that dialogue and the oppressive 'peace' unilaterally imposed by Sybil's father upon his household: although the girl finally accepts the suitor of her father's choice, she does so as an active participant in a courtship whose progress subtly undercuts the inflexible will which 'bids all murmurs, all objections cease'.

The complexity of Crabbe's vision stems not merely from his recognition of the inherent plurality and mutability of the observed world, but also from a heightened consciousness of the multiplicity of vantage-points open to the observer. 'What is a Church?' asks the unspecified interlocutor at the beginning of Letter II of *The Borough*, and the question is answered from three separate points of view before Crabbe proceeds in his own person to represent the building itself, firstly in long architectural perspective and then through a near-microscopic attention to the patterns formed by the lichens on the fabric of the tower; in Letter IX he shows the 'weary rustic' enviously overlooking the activities of the 'joyous crew' on the river below, and then sharply qualifies the watcher's over-simple response by homing in on details misleadingly obscured by distance; while in Letter XXII he achieves a remarkable dramatic effect by suddenly withdrawing from close contemplation of Grimes' mental turmoil to the vantage-point of a summer visitor uncomprehendingly observing the guilt-ridden fisherman's behaviour through a spy-glass. These perceptual shifts tend to work not by a process of cancellation, but cumulatively, towards a multi-faceted representation of the world; and it is clear how appropriate to Crabbe's naturally expansive and accommodating view of life were the narrative forms he adopted, forms which gave him latitude to explore, through the speech and actions of a multitude of diverse characters, the variety of angles from which reality may be approached.

Crabbe's equivocal stance risks a great deal, and one senses in his work a recurrent unease at the protean tendencies of his own mind: the apologetic footnotes which litter *The Borough* reveal with particular clarity a tension between the moralising and the exploratory impulses in him, between his anxiety to present his characters in ways which reinforce an approved ethical code and his desire to follow through, by a process of creative identification, the perplexing ramifications of the human spirit. With the passage of time the moralist gained the upper hand, and this in part explains the general slackening so readily discernible in *Tales of the Hall* and the *Posthumous Tales*; but even there – as for example in those striking lines in the fourth of the *Tales of the Hall* in which Richard describes his fall into the sea in terms which, prefiguring Freudian theory, hint at the volitional element in the apparently accidental – one comes upon the moments of recognition, the startling perceptions of the unsettling but vital complexity which was still for Crabbe, I think, the essential truth of things.

Even his most fervent admirers will admit that Crabbe's poetry is uneven in quality, tending at times to flabbiness and banality, but he has not been well served by the numerous editors who have chosen to present his work as a series of incidental felicities, isolating the details of his broad and involved canvases in such a way as to suggest that his strengths were simply those of an accomplished miniaturist. It was by giving himself scope to register a whole network of dynamic interconnections – between man and woman, between the individual and society, between mankind and Nature – and to represent life as fluid, developmental, that Crabbe achieved his most notable effects; and my own selection, while naturally including many of the glittering descriptive passages for which he is justly admired, is intended to give some idea of the scale demanded by his rich and complex vision.

I have excluded all of Crabbe's epigraphs and most of his footnotes, but have otherwise followed the text of the five-volume *Works* published by John Murray in 1823.

Bibliography

There are three collected editions likely to be fairly readily accessible to the modern reader: the *Life and Poems* of 1834, edited by Crabbe's son and published by John Murray; the *Poems* (1905-07), edited by A.W. Ward and published by the Cambridge University Press; and the *Poetical Works* (1908), edited by A.J. and R.M. Carlyle and published by the Oxford University Press. Howard Mills' complete edition of the 1812 *Tales* (which includes a selection from other poems) was published by Cambridge in 1967.

The 1834 *Life* remains the best biography, though René Huchon's heavily padded *George Crabbe and his Times* (John Murray, 1907) corrects a number of inaccuracies in the younger Crabbe's account.

Arthur Pollard's *Crabbe: The Critical Heritage* (Routledge and Kegan Paul, 1972) is an illuminating collection of eighteenth- and nineteenth-century assessments of the poet's work.

The Village: Book I

The Village Life, and every care that reigns
O'er youthful peasants and declining swains;
What labour yields, and what, that labour past,
Age, in its hour of languor, finds at last;
What form the real picture of the poor,
Demand a song – the Muse can give no more.

    Fled are those times, when, in harmonious strains,
The rustic poet praised his native plains:
No shepherds now, in smooth alternate verse,
Their country's beauty or their nymphs' rehearse;   10
Yet still for these we frame the tender strain,
Still in our lays fond Corydons complain,
And shepherds' boys their amorous pains reveal,
The only pains, alas! they never feel.

    On Mincio's banks, in Cæsar's bounteous reign,
If Tityrus found the Golden Age again,
Must sleepy bards the flattering dream prolong,
Mechanic echoes of the Mantuan song?
From Truth and Nature shall we widely stray,
Where Virgil, not where Fancy, leads the way?   20

    Yes, thus the Muses sing of happy swains,
Because the Muses never knew their pains:
They boast their peasants' pipes; but peasants now
Resign their pipes and plod behind the plough;
And few, amid the rural-tribe, have time
To number syllables, and play with rhyme;
Save honest Duck, what son of verse could share
The poet's rapture, and the peasant's care?
Or the great labours of the field degrade,
With the new peril of a poorer trade?   30

    From this chief cause these idle praises spring,
That themes so easy few forbear to sing;
For no deep thought the trifling subjects ask;

To sing of shepherds is an easy task:
The happy youth assumes the common strain,
A nymph his mistress, and himself a swain;
With no sad scenes he clouds his tuneful prayer,
But all, to look like her, is painted fair.
    I grant indeed that fields and flocks have charms
For him that grazes or for him that farms;   40
But when amid such pleasing scenes I trace
The poor laborious natives of the place,
And see the mid-day sun, with fervid ray,
On their bare heads and dewy temples play;
While some, with feebler heads and fainter hearts,
Deplore their fortune, yet sustain their parts:
Then shall I dare these real ills to hide
In tinsel trappings of poetic pride?
    No; cast by Fortune on a frowning coast,
Which neither groves nor happy valleys boast;   50
Where other cares than those the Muse relates,
And other shepherds dwell with other mates;
By such examples taught, I paint the Cot,
As Truth will paint it, and as Bards will not:
Nor you, ye poor, of letter'd scorn complain,
To you the smoothest song is smooth in vain;
O'ercome by labour, and bow'd down by time,
Feel you the barren flattery of a rhyme?
Can poets soothe you, when you pine for bread,
By winding myrtles round your ruin'd shed?   60
Can their light tales your weighty griefs o'erpower,
Or glad with airy mirth the toilsome hour?
    Lo! where the heath, with withering brake grown o'er,
Lends the light turf that warms the neighbouring poor;
From thence a length of burning sand appears,
Where the thin harvest waves its wither'd ears;
Rank weeds, that every art and care defy,
Reign o'er the land, and rob the blighted rye:
There thistles stretch their prickly arms afar,

18

And to the ragged infant threaten war; 70
There poppies nodding, mock the hope of toil;
There the blue bugloss paints the sterile soil;
Hardy and high, above the slender sheaf,
The slimy mallow waves her silky leaf;
O'er the young shoot the charlock throws a shade,
And clasping tares cling round the sickly blade;
With mingled tints the rocky coasts abound,
And a sad splendour vainly shines around.
So looks the nymph whom wretched arts adorn,
Betray'd by man, then left for man to scorn; 80
Whose cheek in vain assumes the mimic rose,
While her sad eyes the troubled breast disclose;
Whose outward splendour is but folly's dress,
Exposing most, when most it gilds distress.

Here joyless roam a wild amphibious race,
With sullen wo display'd in every face;
Who, far from civil arts and social fly,
And scowl at strangers with suspicious eye.

Here too the lawless merchant of the main
Draws from his plough th'intoxicated swain; 90
Want only claim'd the labour of the day,
But vice now steals his nightly rest away.

Where are the swains, who, daily labour done,
With rural games play'd down the setting sun;
Who struck with matchless force the bounding ball,
Or made the pond'rous quoit obliquely fall;
While some huge Ajax, terrible and strong,
Engaged some artful stripling of the throng,
And fell beneath him, foil'd, while far around
Hoarse triumph rose, and rocks return'd the sound? 100
Where now are these? – Beneath yon cliff they stand,
To show the freighted pinnace where to land;
To load the ready steed with guilty haste,
To fly in terror o'er the pathless waste,
Or, when detected, in their straggling course,

To foil their foes by cunning or by force;
Or, yielding part (which equal knaves demand),
To gain a lawless passport through the land.
    Here, wand'ring long, amid these frowning fields,
I sought the simple life that Nature yields; 110
Rapine and Wrong and Fear usurp'd her place,
And a bold, artful, surly, savage race;
Who, only skill'd to take the finny tribe,
The yearly dinner, or septennial bribe,
Wait on the shore, and, as the waves run high,
On the tost vessel bend their eager eye,
Which to their coast directs its vent'rous way;
Theirs, or the ocean's, miserable prey.
    As on their neighbouring beach yon swallows stand,
And wait for favouring winds to leave the land; 120
While still for flight the ready wing is spread:
So waited I the favouring hour, and fled;
Fled from these shores where guilt and famine reign,
And cried, Ah! hapless they who still remain;
Who still remain to hear the ocean roar,
Whose greedy waves devour the lessening shore;
Till some fierce tide, with more imperious sway,
Sweeps the low hut and all it holds away;
When the sad tenant weeps from door to door,
And begs a poor protection from the poor! 130
    But these are scenes where Nature's niggard hand
Gave a spare portion to the famish'd land;
Hers is the fault, if here mankind complain
Of fruitless toil and labour spent in vain;
But yet in other scenes more fair in view,
Where Plenty smiles – alas! she smiles for few –
And those who taste not, yet behold her store,
Are as the slaves that dig the golden ore,
The wealth around them makes them doubly poor.
    Or will you deem them amply paid in health, 140
Labour's fair child, that languishes with wealth?

Go then! and see them rising with the sun,
Through a long course of daily toil to run;
See them beneath the dog-star's raging heat,
When the knees tremble and the temples beat;
Behold them, leaning on their scythes, look o'er
The labour past, and toils to come explore;
See them alternate suns and showers engage,
And hoard up aches and anguish for their age;
Through fens and marshy moors their steps pursue,   150
When their warm pores imbibe the evening dew;
Then own that labour may as fatal be
To these thy slaves, as thine excess to thee.

    Amid this tribe too oft a manly pride
Strives in strong toil the fainting heart to hide;
There may you see the youth of slender frame
Contend with weakness, weariness, and shame;
Yet, urged along, and proudly loth to yield,
He strives to join his fellows of the field.
Till long-contending nature droops at last,   160
Declining health rejects his poor repast,
His cheerless spouse the coming danger sees,
And mutual murmurs urge the slow disease.

    Yet grant them health, 'tis not for us to tell,
Though the head droops not, that the heart is well;
Or will you praise that homely, healthy fare,
Plenteous and plain, that happy peasants share!
Oh! trifle not with wants you cannot feel,
Nor mock the misery of a stinted meal;
Homely, not wholesome, plain, not plenteous, such   170
As you who praise would never deign to touch.

    Ye gentle souls, who dream of rural ease,
Whom the smooth stream and smoother sonnet please;
Go! if the peaceful cot your praises share,
Go look within, and ask if peace be there;
If peace be his – that drooping weary sire,
Or theirs, that offspring round their feeble fire;

21

Or hers, that matron pale, whose trembling hand
Turns on the wretched hearth th'expiring brand!
Nor yet can Time itself obtain for these   180
Life's latest comforts, due respect and ease;
For yonder see that hoary swain, whose age
Can with no cares except his own engage;
Who, propp'd on that rude staff, looks up to see
The bare arms broken from the withering tree,
On which, a boy, he climb'd the loftiest bough,
Then his first joy, but his sad emblem now.
He once was chief in all the rustic trade;
His steady hand the straightest furrow made;
Full many a prize he won, and still is proud   190
To find the triumphs of his youth allow'd;
A transient pleasure sparkles in his eyes,
He hears and smiles, then thinks again and sighs:
For now he journeys to his grave in pain;
The rich disdain him; nay, the poor disdain:
Alternate masters now their slave command,
Urge the weak efforts of his feeble hand,
And, when his age attempts its task in vain,
With ruthless taunts, of lazy poor complain.
Oft may you see him, when he tends the sheep,   200
His winter-charge, beneath the hillock weep;
Oft hear him murmur to the winds that blow
O'er his white locks and bury them in snow,
When, roused by rage and muttering in the morn,
He mends the broken hedge with icy thorn: –
"Why do I live, when I desire to be
"At once from life and life's long labour free?
"Like leaves in spring, the young are blown away,
"Without the sorrows of a slow decay;
"I, like yon wither'd leaf, remain behind,   210
"Nipp'd by the frost, and shivering in the wind;
"There it abides till younger buds come on,
"As I, now all my fellow-swains are gone;

22

"Then, from the rising generation thrust,
"It falls, like me, unnoticed to the dust.
  "These fruitful fields, these numerous flocks I see,
"Are others' gain, but killing cares to me;
"To me the children of my youth are lords,
"Cool in their looks, but hasty in their words:
"Wants of their own demand their care; and who   220
"Feels his own want and succours others too?
"A lonely, wretched man, in pain I go,
"None need my help, and none relieve my wo;
"Then let my bones beneath the turf be laid,
"And men forget the wretch they would not aid."
  Thus groan the old, till, by disease oppress'd,
They taste a final wo, and then they rest.
  Theirs is yon house that holds the parish-poor,
Whose walls of mud scarce bear the broken door;
There, where the putrid vapours, flagging, play,   230
And the dull wheel hums doleful through the day; —
There children dwell who know no parents' care;
Parents, who know no children's love, dwell there!
Heart-broken matrons on their joyless bed,
Forsaken wives, and mothers never wed;
Dejected widows with unheeded tears,
And crippled age with more than childhood fears;
The lame, the blind, and, far the happiest they!
The moping idiot and the madman gay.
Here too the sick their final doom receive,   240
Here brought, amid the scenes of grief, to grieve,
Where the loud groans from some sad chamber flow,
Mix'd with the clamours of the crowd below;
Here, sorrowing, they each kindred sorrow scan,
And the cold charities of man to man:
Whose laws indeed for ruin'd age provide,
And strong compulsion plucks the scrap from pride;
But still that scrap is bought with many a sigh,
And pride embitters what it can't deny.

23

Say ye, oppress'd by some fantastic woes,   250
Some jarring nerve that baffles your repose;
Who press the downy couch, while slaves advance
With timid eye, to read the distant glance;
Who with sad prayers the weary doctor tease,
To name the nameless ever-new disease;
Who with mock patience dire complaints endure,
Which real pain and that alone can cure;
How would ye bear in real pain to lie,
Despised, neglected, left alone to die?
How would ye bear to draw your latest breath,   260
Where all that's wretched paves the way for death?
    Such is that room which one rude beam divides,
And naked rafters form the sloping sides;
Where the vile bands that bind the thatch are seen,
And lath and mud are all that lie between;
Save one dull pane, that, coarsely patch'd, gives way
To the rude tempest, yet excludes the day:
Here, on a matted flock, with dust o'erspread,
The drooping wretch reclines his languid head;
For him no hand the cordial cup applies,   270
Or wipes the tear that stagnates in his eyes;
No friends with soft discourse his pain beguile,
Or promise hope till sickness wears a smile.
    But soon a loud and hasty summons calls,
Shakes the thin roof, and echoes round the walls;
Anon, a figure enters, quaintly neat,
All pride and business, bustle and conceit;
With looks unalter'd by these scenes of wo,
With speed that, entering, speaks his haste to go,
He bids the gazing throng around him fly,   280
And carries fate and physic in his eye:
A potent quack, long versed in human ills,
Who first insults the victim whom he kills;
Whose murd'rous hand a drowsy Bench protect,
And whose most tender mercy is neglect.

24

Paid by the parish for attendance here,
He wears contempt upon his sapient sneer;
In haste he seeks the bed where Misery lies,
Impatience mark'd in his averted eyes;
And, some habitual queries hurried o'er,   290
Without reply, he rushes on the door:
His drooping patient, long inured to pain,
And long unheeded, knows remonstrance vain;
He ceases now the feeble help to crave
Of man; and silent sinks into the grave.

But ere his death some pious doubts arise,
Some simple fears, which "bold bad" men despise;
Fain would he ask the parish-priest to prove
His title certain to the joys above:
For this he sends the murmuring nurse, who calls   300
The holy stranger to these dismal walls:
And doth not he, the pious man, appear,
He, "passing rich with forty pounds a year?"
Ah! no; a shepherd of a different stock,
And far unlike him, feeds this little flock:
A jovial youth, who thinks his Sunday's task
As much as God or man can fairly ask;
The rest he gives to loves and labours light,
To fields the morning, and to feasts the night;
None better skill'd the noisy pack to guide,   310
To urge their chase, to cheer them or to chide;
A sportsman keen, he shoots through half the day,
And, skill'd at whist, devotes the night to play:
Then, while such honours bloom around his head,
Shall he sit sadly by the sick man's bed,
To raise the hope he feels not, or with zeal
To combat fears that e'en the pious feel?

Now once again the gloomy scene explore,
Less gloomy now; the bitter hour is o'er,
The man of many sorrows sighs no more. –   320
Up yonder hill, behold how sadly slow

25

The bier moves winding from the vale below;
There lie the happy dead, from trouble free,
And the glad parish pays the frugal fee:
No more, O Death! thy victim starts to hear
Churchwarden stern, or kingly overseer;
No more the farmer claims his humble bow,
Thou art his lord, the best of tyrants thou!
    Now to the church behold the mourners come,
Sedately torpid and devoutly dumb;   330
The village children now their games suspend,
To see the bier that bears their ancient friend:
For he was one in all their idle sport,
And like a monarch ruled their little court;
The pliant bow he form'd, the flying ball,
The bat, the wicket, were his labours all;
Him now they follow to his grave, and stand
Silent and sad, and gazing, hand in hand;
While bending low, their eager eyes explore
The mingled relics of the parish poor: 340
The bell tolls late, the moping owl flies round,
Fear marks the flight and magnifies the sound;
The busy priest, detain'd by weightier care,
Defers his duty till the day of prayer;
And, waiting long, the crowd retire distress'd,
To think a poor man's bones should lie unbless'd.

The Parish Register

from *The Introduction*

To every cot the lord's indulgent mind   129
Has a small space for garden-ground assign'd;
Here – till return of morn dismiss'd the farm –
The careful peasant plies the sinewy arm,
Warm'd as he works, and casts his look around
On every foot of that improving ground:
It is his own he sees; his master's eye
Peers not about, some secret fault to spy;
Nor voice severe is there, nor censure known; –
Hope, profit, pleasure, – they are all his own.
Here grow the humble cives, and, hard by them,
The leek with crown globose and reedy stem;   140
High climb his pulse in many an even row,
Deep strike the ponderous roots in soil below;
And herbs of potent smell and pungent taste
Give a warm relish to the night's repast.
Apples and cherries grafted by his hand,
And cluster'd nuts for neighbouring market stand.
    Nor thus concludes his labour; near the cot,
The reed-fence rises round some fav'rite spot;
Where rich carnations, pinks with purple eyes,
Proud hyacinths, the least some florist's prize,   150
Tulips tall-stemm'd and pounced auriculas rise.
    Here on a Sunday-eve, when service ends,
Meet and rejoice a family of friends;
All speak aloud, are happy and are free,
And glad they seem, and gaily they agree.
    What, though fastidious ears may shun the speech,
Where all are talkers and where none can teach;
Where still the welcome and the words are old,
And the same stories are for ever told;

Yet theirs is joy that, bursting from the heart,   160
Prompts the glad tongue these nothings to impart;
That forms these tones of gladness we despise,
That lifts their steps, that sparkles in their eyes;
That talks or laughs or runs or shouts or plays,
And speaks in all their looks and all their ways.

Fair scenes of peace! ye might detain us long,
But vice and misery now demand the song;
And turn our view from dwellings simply neat,
To this infected row, we term our street.

Here, in cabal, a disputatious crew   170
Each evening meet; the sot, the cheat, the shrew:
Riots are nightly heard: – the curse, the cries
Of beaten wife, perverse in her replies;
While shrieking children hold each threat'ning hand,
And sometimes life, and sometimes food demand:
Boys, in their first-stol'n rags, to swear begin,
And girls, who heed not dress, are skill'd in gin:
Snarers and smugglers here their gains divide;
Ensnaring females here their victims hide;
And here is one, the sibyl of the row,   180
Who knows all secrets, or affects to know.
Seeking their fate, to her the simple run,
To her the guilty, theirs awhile to shun;
Mistress of worthless arts, depraved in will,
Her care unbless'd and unrepaid her skill,
Slave to the tribe, to whose command she stoops,
And poorer than the poorest maid she dupes.

Between the road-way and the walls, offence
Invades all eyes and strikes on every sense:
There lie, obscene, at every open door,   190
Heaps from the hearth and sweepings from the floor,
And day by day the mingled masses grow,
As sinks are disembogued and kennels flow.

There hungry dogs from hungry children steal,
There pigs and chickens quarrel for a meal;

There dropsied infants wail without redress,
And all is want and wo and wretchedness:
Yet should these boys, with bodies bronzed and bare,
High-swoln and hard, outlive that lack of care –
Forced on some farm, the unexerted strength,   200
Though loth to action, is compell'd at length,
When warm'd by health, as serpents in the spring,
Aside their slough of indolence they fling.

  Yet, ere they go, a greater evil comes –
See! crowded beds in those contiguous rooms;
Beds but ill parted, by a paltry screen
Of paper'd lath or curtain dropp'd between;
Daughters and sons to yon compartments creep,
And parents here beside their children sleep:
Ye who have power, these thoughtless people part,   210
Nor let the ear be first to taint the heart.

  Come! search within, nor sight nor smell regard;
The true physician walks the foulest ward.
See! on the floor what frouzy patches rest!
What nauseous fragments on yon fractured chest!
What downy dust beneath yon window-seat!
And round these posts that serve this bed for feet;
This bed where all those tatter'd garments lie,
Worn by each sex, and now perforce thrown by!

  See! as we gaze, an infant lifts its head,   220
Left by neglect and burrow'd in that bed;
The mother-gossip has the love suppress'd
An infant's cry once waken'd in her breast;
And daily prattles, as her round she takes,
(With strong resentment) of the want she makes.

  Whence all these woes? – From want of virtuous will,
Of honest shame, of time-improving skill;
From want of care t'employ the vacant hour,
And want of ev'ry kind but want of power.

  Here are no wheels for either wool or flax,   230
But packs of cards – made up of sundry packs;

Here is no clock, nor will they turn the glass,
And see how swift th'important moments pass;
Here are no books, but ballads on the wall,
Are some abusive, and indecent all;
Pistols are here, unpair'd; with nets and hooks,
Of every kind, for rivers, ponds, and brooks;
An ample flask, that nightly rovers fill
With recent poison from the Dutchman's still;
A box of tools, with wires of various size,   240
Frocks, wigs, and hats, for night or day disguise,
And bludgeons stout to gain or guard a prize.
   To every house belongs a space of ground,
Of equal size, once fenced with paling round;
That paling now by slothful waste destroy'd,
Dead gorse and stumps of elder fill the void;
Save in the centre-spot, whose walls of clay
Hide sots and striplings at their drink or play:
Within, a board, beneath a tiled retreat,
Allures the bubble and maintains the cheat;   250
Where heavy ale in spots like varnish shows,
Where chalky tallies yet remain in rows;
Black pipes and broken jugs the seats defile,
The walls and windows, rhymes and reck'nings vile;
Prints of the meanest kind disgrace the door,
And cards, in curses torn, lie fragments on the floor.
   Here his poor bird th'inhuman cocker brings,
Arms his hard heel and clips his golden wings;
With spicy food th'impatient spirit feeds,
And shouts and curses as the battle bleeds.   260
Struck through the brain, deprived of both his eyes,
The vanquish'd bird must combat till he dies;
Must faintly peck at his victorious foe,
And reel and stagger at each feeble blow:
When fall'n, the savage grasps his dabbled plumes,
His blood-stain'd arms, for other deaths assumes;

And damns the craven-fowl, that lost his stake,
And only bled and perish'd for his sake.   268

from *Baptisms*

Next, with their boy, a decent couple came,   403
And call'd him Robert, 'twas his father's name;
Three girls preceded, all by time endear'd,
And future births were neither hoped nor fear'd:
Bless'd in each other, but to no excess;
Health, quiet, comfort, form'd their happiness;
Love all made up of torture and delight,
Was but mere madness in this couple's sight: 410
Susan could think, though not without a sigh,
If she were gone, who should her place supply;
And Robert, half in earnest, half in jest,
Talk of her spouse when he should be at rest:
Yet strange would either think it to be told,
Their love was cooling or their hearts were cold.
Few were their acres, – but, with these content,
They were, each pay-day, ready with their rent:
And few their wishes – what their farm denied,
The neighbouring town, at trifling cost, supplied.   420
If at the draper's window Susan cast
A longing look, as with her goods she pass'd,
And, with the produce of the wheel and churn,
Bought her a Sunday-robe on her return;
True to her maxim, she would take no rest,
Till care repaid that portion to the chest:
Or if, when loitering at the Whitsun-fair,
Her Robert spent some idle shillings there;
Up at the barn, before the break of day,
He made his labour for th'indulgence pay: 430
Thus both – that waste itself might work in vain –

31

Wrought double tides, and all was well again.
　　Yet, though so prudent, there were times of joy,
(The day they wed, the christening of the boy,)
When to the wealthier farmers there was shown
Welcome unfeign'd, and plenty like their own;
For Susan served the great, and had some pride
Among our topmost people to preside:
Yet in that plenty, in that welcome free,
There was the guiding nice frugality,　　　　　　　　　　440
That, in the festal as the frugal day,
Has, in a different mode, a sovereign sway;
As tides the same attractive influence know,
In the least ebb and in their proudest flow;
The wise frugality, that does not give
A life to saving, but that saves to live;
Sparing, not pinching, mindful though not mean,
O'er all presiding, yet in nothing seen.　　　　　　　　　448

from *Marriages*

　　For Lucy Collins happier days had been,　　　　　　313
Had Footman Daniel scorn'd his native green;
Or when he came an idle coxcomb down,
Had he his love reserved for lass in town;
To Stephen Hill she then had pledged her truth, –
A sturdy, sober, kind, unpolish'd youth;
But from the day, that fatal day she spied
The pride of Daniel, Daniel was her pride.　　　　　　320
In all concerns was Stephen just and true;
But coarse his doublet was and patch'd in view,
And felt his stockings were, and blacker than his shoe;
While Daniel's linen all was fine and fair, –
His master wore it, and he deign'd to wear:
(To wear his livery, some respect might prove;

32

To wear his linen, must be sign of love:)
Blue was his coat, unsoil'd by spot or stain;
His hose were silk, his shoes of Spanish-grain;
A silver knot his breadth of shoulder bore;   330
A diamond buckle blazed his breast before –
Diamond he swore it was! and show'd it as he swore;
Rings on his fingers shone; his milk-white hand
Could pick-tooth case and box for snuff command:
And thus, with clouded cane, a fop complete,
He stalk'd, the jest and glory of the street.
Join'd with these powers, he could so sweetly sing,
Talk with such toss, and saunter with such swing;
Laugh with such glee, and trifle with such art,
That Lucy's promise fail'd to shield her heart.   340
    Stephen, meantime, to ease his amorous cares,
Fix'd his full mind upon his farm's affairs;
Two pigs, a cow, and wethers half a score,
Increased his stock, and still he look'd for more.
He, for his acres few, so duly paid,
That yet more acres to his lot were laid;
Till our chaste nymphs no longer felt disdain,
And prudent matrons praised the frugal swain;
Who thriving well, through many a fruitful year,
Now clothed himself anew, and acted overseer.   350
    Just then poor Lucy, from her friend in town,
Fled in pure fear, and came a beggar down;
Trembling, at Stephen's door she knock'd for bread, –
Was chidden first, next pitied, and then fed;
Then sat at Stephen's board, then shared in Stephen's bed:
All hope of marriage lost in her disgrace,
He mourns a flame revived, and she a love of lace.   357

from *Burials*

Next died the Lady who yon Hall possess'd;   233
And here they brought her noble bones to rest.
In Town she dwelt; – forsaken stood the Hall:
Worms ate the floors, the tap'stry fled the wall:
No fire the kitchen's cheerless grate display'd;
No cheerful light the long-closed sash convey'd;
The crawling worm, that turns a summer-fly,
Here spun his shroud and laid him up to die   240
The winter-death: – upon the bed of state,
The bat shrill-shrieking woo'd his flickering mate;
To empty rooms the curious came no more,
From empty cellars turn'd the angry poor,
And surly beggars cursed the ever-bolted door.
To one small room the steward found his way,
Where tenants follow'd to complain and pay;
Yet no complaint before the Lady came,
The feeling servant spared the feeble dame;
Who saw her farms with his observing eyes,   250
And answer'd all requests with his replies: –
She came not down, her falling groves to view;
Why should she know, what one so faithful knew?
Why come, from many clamorous tongues to hear,
What one so just might whisper in her ear?
Her oaks or acres, why with care explore;
Why learn the wants, the sufferings of the poor;
When one so knowing all their worth could trace,
And one so piteous govern'd in her place?
Lo! now, what dismal sons of Darkness come,   260
To bear this daughter of Indulgence home;
Tragedians all, and well arranged in black!
Who nature, feeling, force, expression lack;
Who cause no tear, but gloomily pass by,
And shake their sables in the wearied eye,
That turns disgusted from the pompous scene,

Proud without grandeur, with profusion, mean!
The tear for kindness past affection owes;
For worth deceased the sigh from reason flows;
E'en well-feign'd passion for our sorrows call,   270
And real tears for mimic miseries fall:
But this poor farce has neither truth nor art,
To please the fancy or to touch the heart;
Unlike the darkness of the sky, that pours
On the dry ground its fertilizing showers;
Unlike to that which strikes the soul with dread,
When thunders roar and forky fires are shed;
Dark but not awful, dismal but yet mean,
With anxious bustle moves the cumbrous scene;
Presents no objects tender or profound,   280
But spreads its cold unmeaning gloom around.
      When woes are feign'd, how ill such forms appear;
And oh! how needless, when the wo's sincere.
      Slow to the vault they come, with heavy tread,
Bending beneath the Lady and her lead;
A case of elm surrounds that ponderous chest,
Close on that case the crimson velvet's press'd;
Ungenerous this, that to the worm denies,
With niggard-caution, his appointed prize;
For now, ere yet he works his tedious way,   290
Through cloth and wood and metal to his prey,
That prey dissolving shall a mass remain,
That fancy loathes and worms themselves disdain.
      But see! the master-mourner makes his way,
To end his office for the coffin'd clay;
Pleased that our rustic men and maids behold
His plate like silver, and his studs like gold,
As they approach to spell the age, the name,
And all the titles of th'illustrious dame. –
This as (my duty done) some scholar read,   300
A village-father look'd disdain and said:
"Away, my friends! why take such pains to know

"What some brave marble soon in church shall show?
"Where not alone her gracious name shall stand,
"But how she lived – the blessing of the land;
"How much we all deplored the noble dead,
"What groans we utter'd and what tears we shed;
"Tears, true as those, which in the sleepy eyes
"Of weeping cherubs on the stone shall rise;
"Tears, true as those, which, ere she found her grave,   310
"The noble Lady to our sorrows gave."

                                    *

    Down by the church-way walk and where the brook
Winds round the chancel like a shepherd's crook;
In that small house, with those green pales before,
Where jasmine trails on either side the door;
Where those dark shrubs that now grow wild at will,
Were clipp'd in form and tantalized with skill;
Where cockles blanch'd and pebbles neatly spread,
Form'd shining borders for the larkspurs' bed; –
There lived a Lady, wise, austere, and nice,   320
Who show'd her virtue by her scorn of vice;
In the dear fashions of her youth she dress'd,
A pea-green Joseph was her favourite vest;
Erect she stood, she walk'd with stately mien,
Tight was her length of stays, and she was tall and lean.
    There long she lived in maiden-state immured,
From looks of love and treacherous man secured;
Though evil fame – (but that was long before)
Had blown her dubious blast at Catherine's door:
A Captain thither, rich from India came,   330
And though a cousin call'd, it touch'd her fame:
Her annual stipend rose from his behest,
And all the long-prized treasures she possess'd: –
If aught like joy awhile appear'd to stay
In that stern face, and chase those frowns away;
'Twas when her treasures she disposed for view,
And heard the praises to their splendour due;

Silks beyond price, so rich, they'd stand alone,
And diamonds blazing on the buckled zone;
Rows of rare pearls by curious workmen set,   340
And bracelets fair in box of glossy jet;
Bright polish'd amber precious from its size,
Or forms the fairest fancy could devise:
Her drawers of cedar, shut with secret springs,
Conceal'd the watch of gold and rubied rings;
Letters, long proofs of love, and verses fine
Round the pink'd rims of crisped Valentine.
Her china-closet, cause of daily care,
For woman's wonder held her pencill'd ware;
That pictured wealth of China and Japan,   350
Like its cold mistress, shunn'd the eye of man.
    Her neat small room, adorn'd with maiden-taste,
A clipp'd French puppy, first of favourites, graced:
A parrot next, but dead and stuff'd with art;
(For Poll, when living, lost the Lady's heart,
And then his life; for he was heard to speak
Such frightful words as tinged his Lady's cheek:)
Unhappy bird! who had no power to prove,
Save by such speech, his gratitude and love.
A grey old cat his whiskers lick'd beside;   360
A type of sadness in the house of pride.
The polish'd surface of an India chest,
A glassy globe, in frame of ivory, press'd;
Where swam two finny creatures; one of gold,
Of silver one; both beauteous to behold: –
All these were form'd the guiding taste to suit;
The beasts well-manner'd and the fishes mute.
A widow'd Aunt was there, compell'd by need
The nymph to flatter and her tribe to feed;
Who, veiling well her scorn, endured the clog,   370
Mute as the fish and fawning as the dog.
    As years increased, these treasures, her delight,
Arose in value in their owner's sight:

37

A miser knows that, view it as he will,
A guinea kept is but a guinea still;
And so he puts it to its proper use,
That something more this guinea may produce:
But silks and rings, in the possessor's eyes,
The oft'ner seen, the more in value rise,
And thus are wisely hoarded to bestow   380
The kind of pleasure that with years will grow.

    But what avail'd their worth – if worth had they, –
In the sad summer of her slow decay?

    Then we beheld her turn an anxious look
From trunks and chests, and fix it on her book, –
A rich-bound Book of Prayer the Captain gave,
(Some Princess had it, or was said to have;)
And then once more, on all her stores, look round,
And draw a sigh so piteous and profound,
That told, "Alas! how hard from these to part,   390
"And for new hopes and habits form the heart!
"What shall I do, (she cried) my peace of mind
"To gain in dying, and to die resign'd?"

    "Hear," we return'd; – "these baubles cast aside,
"Nor give thy God a rival in thy pride;
"Thy closets shut, and ope thy kitchen's door;
"*There* own thy failings, *here* invite the poor;
"A friend of Mammon let thy bounty make;
"For widows' prayers, thy vanities forsake;
"And let the hungry, of thy pride, partake: 400
"Then shall thy inward eye with joy survey
"The angel Mercy tempering Death's delay!"

    Alas! 'twas hard; the treasures still had charms,
Hope still its flattery, sickness its alarms;
Still was the same unsettled, clouded view,
And the same plaintive cry, "What shall I do?"

    Nor change appear'd: for when her race was run,
Doubtful we all exclaim'd, "What has been done?"
Apart she lived, and still she lies alone;

Yon earthy heap awaits the flattering stone,   410
On which invention shall be long employ'd,
To show the various worth of Catherine Lloyd.

The Borough

LETTER I
General Description

"Describe the Borough" – though our idle tribe
May love description, can we so describe,
That you shall fairly streets and buildings trace,
And all that gives distinction to a place?
This cannot be; yet, moved by your request,
A part I paint – let fancy form the rest.
   Cities and towns, the various haunts of men,
Require the pencil; they defy the pen:
Could he, who sang so well the Grecian fleet,
So well have sung of alley, lane, or street?   10
Can measured lines these various buildings show,
The Town-Hall Turning, or the Prospect Row?
Can I the seats of wealth and want explore,
And lengthen out my lays from door to door?
   Then let thy fancy aid me – I repair
From this tall mansion of our last-year's mayor,
Till we the outskirts of the Borough reach,
And these half-buried buildings next the beach;
Where hang at open doors the net and cork,
While squalid sea-dames mend the meshy work;   20
Till comes the hour, when fishing through the tide,
The weary husband throws his freight aside;
A living mass, which now demands the wife,
Th'alternate labours of their humble life.
   Can scenes like these withdraw thee from thy wood,
Thy upland forest or thy valley's flood?
Seek then thy garden's shrubby bound, and look,
As it steals by, upon the bordering brook;
That winding streamlet, limpid, lingering, slow,
Where the reeds whisper when the zephyrs blow;   30

Where in the midst, upon her throne of green,
Sits the large lily as the water's queen;
And makes the current, forced awhile to stay,
Murmur and bubble as it shoots away;
Draw then the strongest contrast to that stream,
And our broad river will before thee seem.

   With ceaseless motion comes and goes the tide,
Flowing, it fills the channel vast and wide;
Then back to sea, with strong majestic sweep
It rolls, in ebb yet terrible and deep;   40
Here sampire-banks and salt-wort bound the flood,
There stakes and sea-weeds withering on the mud;
And higher up, a ridge of all things base,
Which some strong tide has roll'd upon the place.

   Thy gentle river boasts its pygmy boat,
Urged on by pains, half-grounded, half afloat;
While at her stern an angler takes his stand,
And marks the fish he purposes to land;
From that clear space, where, in the cheerful ray
Of the warm sun, the scaly people play.   50

   Far other craft our prouder river shows,
Hoys, pinks and sloops; brigs, brigantines and snows:
Nor angler we on our wide stream descry,
But one poor dredger where his oysters lie:
He, cold and wet, and driving with the tide,
Beats his weak arms against his tarry side,
Then drains the remnant of diluted gin,
To aid the warmth that languishes within;
Renewing oft his poor attempts to beat
His tingling fingers into gathering heat.   60

   He shall again be seen when evening comes,
And social parties crowd their favourite rooms:
Where on the table pipes and papers lie,
The steaming bowl or foaming tankard by;
'Tis then, with all these comforts spread around,
They hear the painful dredger's welcome sound;

And few themselves the savoury boon deny,
The food that feeds, the living luxury.

    Yon is our quay! those smaller hoys from town,
Its various wares, for country-use, bring down;   70
Those laden waggons, in return, impart
The country-produce to the city mart;
Hark! to the clamour in that miry road,
Bounded and narrow'd by yon vessels' load;
The lumbering wealth she empties round the place,
Package, and parcel, hogshead, chest, and case:
While the loud seaman and the angry hind,
Mingling in business, bellow to the wind.

    Near these a crew amphibious, in the docks,
Rear, for the sea, those castles on the stocks: 80
See! the long keel, which soon the waves must hide;
See! the strong ribs which form the roomy side;
Bolts yielding slowly to the sturdiest stroke,
And planks which curve and crackle in the smoke.
Around the whole rise cloudy wreaths, and far
Bear the warm pungence of o'er-boiling tar.

    Dabbling on shore half-naked sea-boys crowd,
Swim round a ship, or swing upon the shroud;
Or in a boat purloin'd, with paddles play,
And grow familiar with the watery way: 90
Young though they be, they feel whose sons they are,
They know what British seamen do and dare;
Proud of that fame, they raise and they enjoy
The rustic wonder of the village-boy.

    Before you bid these busy scenes adieu,
Behold the wealth that lies in public view,
Those far-extended heaps of coal and coke,
Where fresh-fill'd lime-kilns breathe their stifling smoke.
This shall pass off, and you behold, instead,
The night-fire gleaming on its chalky bed;   100
When from the light-house brighter beams will rise,
To show the shipman where the shallow lies.

Thy walks are ever pleasant; every scene
Is rich in beauty, lively, or serene –
Rich – is that varied view with woods around,
Seen from the seat, within the shrubb'ry bound;
Where shines the distant lake, and where appear
From ruins bolting, unmolested deer;
Lively – the village-green, the inn, the place,
Where the good widow schools her infant race.   110
Shops, whence are heard the hammer and the saw,
And village-pleasures unreproved by law;
Then how serene! when in your favourite room,
Gales from your jasmines soothe the evening gloom;
When from your upland paddock you look down,
And just perceive the smoke which hides the town;
When weary peasants at the close of day
Walk to their cots, and part upon the way;
When cattle slowly cross the shallow brook,
And shepherds pen their folds, and rest upon their crook.   120
    We prune our hedges, prime our slender trees,
And nothing looks untutor'd and at ease;
On the wide heath, or in the flow'ry vale,
We scent the vapours of the sea-born gale;
Broad-beaten paths lead on from stile to stile,
And sewers from streets, the road-side banks defile;
Our guarded fields a sense of danger show,
Where garden-crops with corn and clover grow;
Fences are form'd of wreck and placed around,
(With tenters tipp'd) a strong repulsive bound;   130
Wide and deep ditches by the gardens run,
And there in ambush lie the trap and gun;
Or yon broad board, which guards each tempting prize,
"Like a tall bully, lifts its head and lies."
    There stands a cottage with an open door,
Its garden undefended blooms before:
Her wheel is still, and overturn'd her stool,
While the lone widow seeks the neighb'ring pool:

This gives us hope, all views of town to shun –
No! here are tokens of the sailor-son;   140
That old blue jacket, and that shirt of check,
And silken kerchief for the seaman's neck;
Sea-spoils and shells from many a distant shore,
And furry robe from frozen Labrador.
 Our busy streets and sylvan-walks between,
Fen, marshes, bog and heath all intervene;
Here pits of crag, with spongy, plashy base,
To some enrich th'uncultivated space:
For there are blossoms rare, and curious rush,
The gale's rich balm, and sun-dew's crimson blush, 150
Whose velvet leaf with radiant beauty dress'd,
Forms a gay pillow for the plover's breast.
 Not distant far, a house commodious made,
(Lonely yet public stands) for Sunday-trade;
Thither, for this day free, gay parties go,
Their tea-house walk, their tippling rendezvous;
There humble couples sit in corner-bowers,
Or gaily ramble for th'allotted hours;
Sailors and lasses from the town attend,
The servant-lover, the apprentice-friend;   160
With all the idle social tribes who seek,
And find their humble pleasures once a week.
 Turn to the watery world! – but who to thee
(A wonder yet unview'd) shall paint – the sea?
Various and vast, sublime in all its forms,
When lull'd by zephyrs, or when roused by storms,
Its colours changing, when from clouds and sun
Shades after shades upon the surface run;
Embrown'd and horrid now, and now serene,
In limpid blue, and evanescent green;   170
And oft the foggy banks on ocean lie,
Lift the fair sail, and cheat th'experienced eye.
 Be it the summer-noon: a sandy space
The ebbing tide has left upon its place;

Then just the hot and stony beach above,
Light twinkling streams in bright confusion move;
(For heated thus, the warmer air ascends,
And with the cooler in its fall contends) –
Then the broad bosom of the ocean keeps
An equal motion; swelling as it sleeps,   180
Then slowly sinking; curling to the strand,
Faint, lazy waves o'ercreep the ridgy sand,
Or tap the tarry boat with gentle blow,
And back return in silence, smooth and slow.
Ships in the calm seem anchor'd; for they glide
On the still sea, urged solely by the tide;
Art thou not present, this calm scene before,
Where all beside is pebbly length of shore,
And far as eye can reach, it can discern no more?
     Yet sometimes comes a ruffling cloud to make   190
The quiet surface of the ocean shake;
As an awaken'd giant with a frown
Might show his wrath, and then to sleep sink down.
     View now the winter-storm! above, one cloud,
Black and unbroken, all the skies o'ershroud;
Th'unwieldy porpoise through the day before
Had roll'd in view of boding men on shore;
And sometimes hid and sometimes show'd his form,
Dark as the cloud, and furious as the storm.
     All where the eye delights, yet dreads to roam,   200
The breaking billows cast the flying foam
Upon the billows rising – all the deep
Is restless change; the waves so swell'd and steep,
Breaking and sinking, and the sunken swells,
Nor one, one moment, in its station dwells:
But nearer land you may the billows trace,
As if contending in their watery chase;
May watch the mightiest till the shoal they reach,
Then break and hurry to their utmost stretch;
Curl'd as they come, they strike with furious force,   210

45

And then re-flowing, take their grating course,
Raking the rounded flints, which ages past
Roll'd by their rage, and shall to ages last.
    Far off the petrel in the troubled way
Swims with her brood, or flutters in the spray;
She rises often, often drops again,
And sports at ease on the tempestuous main.
    High o'er the restless deep, above the reach
Of gunner's hope, vast flights of wild-ducks stretch;
Far as the eye can glance on either side,   220
In a broad space and level line they glide;
All in their wedge-like figures from the north,
Day after day, flight after flight, go forth.
    In-shore their passage tribes of sea-gulls urge,
And drop for prey within the sweeping surge;
Oft in the rough opposing blast they fly
Far back, then turn, and all their force apply,
While to the storm they give their weak complaining cry;
Or clap the sleek white pinion to the breast,
And in the restless ocean dip for rest.   230
    Darkness begins to reign; the louder wind
Appals the weak and awes the firmer mind;
But frights not him, whom evening and the spray
In part conceal – yon prowler on his way:
Lo! he has something seen; he runs apace,
As if he fear'd companion in the chase;
He sees his prize, and now he turns again,
Slowly and sorrowing – "Was your search in vain?"
Gruffly he answers, "'Tis a sorry sight!
"A seaman's body: there'll be more to-night!"   240
    Hark! to those sounds! they're from distress at sea:
How quick they come! What terrors may there be!
Yes, 'tis a driven vessel: I discern
Lights, signs of terror, gleaming from the stern;
Others behold them too, and from the town
In various parties seamen hurry down;

46

Their wives pursue, and damsels urged by dread,
Lest men so dear be into danger led;
Their head the gown has hooded, and their call
In this sad night is piercing like the squall;   250
They feel their kinds of power, and when they meet,
Chide, fondle, weep, dare, threaten, or entreat.
　　See one poor girl, all terror and alarm,
Has fondly seized upon her lover's arm;
"Thou shalt not venture;" and he answers "No!
"I will not" – still she cries, "Thou shalt not go."
　　No need of this; not here the stoutest boat
Can through such breakers, o'er such billows float;
Yet may they view these lights upon the beach,
Which yield them hope, whom help can never reach.   260
　　From parted clouds the moon her radiance throws
On the wild waves, and all the danger shows;
But shows them beaming in her shining vest,
Terrific splendour! gloom in glory dress'd!
This for a moment, and then clouds again
Hide every beam, and fear and darkness reign.
　　But hear we now those sounds? Do lights appear?
I see them not! the storm alone I hear:
And lo! the sailors homeward take their way;
Man must endure – let us submit and pray.   270
　　Such are our winter-views; but night comes on –
Now business sleeps, and daily cares are gone;
Now parties form, and some their friends assist
To waste the idle hours at sober whist;
The tavern's pleasure or the concert's charm
Unnumber'd moments of their sting disarm;
Play-bills and open doors a crowd invite,
To pass off one dread portion of the night;
And show and song and luxury combined,
Lift off from man this burthen of mankind.   280
　　Others advent'rous walk abroad and meet
Returning parties pacing through the street;

47

When various voices, in the dying day,
Hum in our walks, and greet us in our way;
When tavern-lights flit on from room to room,
And guide the tippling sailor staggering home:
There as we pass, the jingling bells betray
How business rises with the closing day:
Now walking silent, by the river's side,
The ear perceives the rippling of the tide; 290
Or measured cadence of the lads who tow
Some enter'd hoy, to fix her in her row;
Or hollow sound, which from the parish-bell
To some departed spirit bids farewell!
    Thus shall you something of our Borough know,
Far as a verse, with Fancy's aid, can show;
Of sea or river, of a quay or street,
The best description must be incomplete;
But when a happier theme succeeds, and when
Men are our subjects and the deeds of men; 300
Then may we find the Muse in happier style,
And we may sometimes sigh and sometimes smile.

LETTER IX
Amusements

Of our amusements ask you? – We amuse
Ourselves and friends with sea-side walks and views,
Or take a morning ride, a novel, or the news;
Or, seeking nothing, glide about the street,
And so engaged, with various parties meet;
Awhile we stop, discourse of wind and tide,
Bathing and books, the raffle, and the ride:
Thus, with the aid which shops and sailing give,
Life passes on; 'tis labour, but we live.
    When evening comes, our invalids awake, 10

Nerves cease to tremble, heads forbear to ache;
Then cheerful meals the sunken spirits raise,
Cards or the dance, wine, visiting, or plays.
  Soon as the season comes, and crowds arrive,
To their superior rooms the wealthy drive;
Others look round for lodging snug and small,
Such is their taste – they've hatred to a hall;
Hence one his fav'rite habitation gets,
The brick-floor'd parlour which the butcher lets;
Where, through his single light, he may regard   20
The various business of a common yard,
Bounded by backs of buildings form'd of clay,
By stable, sties, and coops, et-cætera.
  The needy-vain, themselves awhile to shun,
For dissipation to these dog-holes run;
Where each (assuming petty pomp) appears,
And quite forgets the shopboard and the shears.
  For them are cheap amusements: they may slip
Beyond the town and take a private dip;
When they may urge that, to be safe they mean,   30
They've heard there's danger in a light machine;
They too can gratis move the quays about,
And gather kind replies to every doubt;
There they a pacing, lounging tribe may view,
The stranger's guides, who've little else to do;
The Borough's placemen, where no more they gain
Than keeps them idle, civil, poor, and vain.
Then may the poorest with the wealthy look
On ocean, glorious page of Nature's book!
May see its varying views in every hour,   40
All softness now, then rising with all power,
As sleeping to invite, or threat'ning to devour:
'Tis this which gives us all our choicest views;
Its waters heal us, and its shores amuse.
  See! those fair nymphs upon that rising strand,
Yon long salt lake has parted from the land;

Well pleased to press that path, so clean, so pure,
To seem in danger, yet to feel secure;
Trifling with terror, while they strive to shun
The curling billows; laughing as they run;   50
They know the neck that joins the shore and sea,
Or, ah! how changed that fearless laugh would be.
    Observe how various parties take their way,
By sea-side walks, or make the sand-hills gay;
There group'd are laughing maids and sighing swains,
And some apart who feel unpitied pains;
Pains from diseases, pains which those who feel,
To the physician, not the fair, reveal:
For nymphs (propitious to the lover's sigh)
Leave these poor patients to complain and die.   60
    Lo! where on that huge anchor sadly leans
That sick tall figure, lost in other scenes;
He late from India's clime impatient sail'd,
There, as his fortune grew, his spirits fail'd;
For each delight, in search of wealth he went,
For ease alone, the wealth acquired is spent –
And spent in vain; enrich'd, aggrieved, he sees
The envied poor possess'd of joy and ease:
And now he flies from place to place, to gain
Strength for enjoyment, and still flies in vain: 70
Mark! with what sadness, of that pleasant crew,
Boist'rous in mirth, he takes a transient view;
And fixing then his eye upon the sea,
Thinks what has been and what must shortly be:
Is it not strange that man should health destroy,
For joys that come when he is dead to joy?
    Now is it pleasant in the summer-eve,
When a broad shore retiring waters leave,
Awhile to wait upon the firm fair sand,
When all is calm at sea, all still at land;   80
And there the ocean's produce to explore,
As floating by, or rolling on the shore;

Those living jellies which the flesh inflame,
Fierce as a nettle, and from that its name;
Some in huge masses, some that you may bring
In the small compass of a lady's ring;
Figured by hand divine – there's not a gem
Wrought by man's art to be compared to them;
Soft, brilliant, tender, through the wave they glow,
And make the moonbeam brighter where they flow.   90
Involved in sea-wrack, here you find a race,
Which science doubting, knows not where to place;
On shell or stone is dropp'd the embryo-seed,
And quickly vegetates a vital breed.

While thus with pleasing wonder you inspect
Treasures the vulgar in their scorn reject,
See as they float along th'entangled weeds
Slowly approach, upborne on bladdery beads;
Wait till the land, and you shall then behold
The fiery sparks those tangled fronds infold,   100
Myriads of living points; th'unaided eye
Can but the fire and not the form descry.
And now your view upon the ocean turn,
And there the splendour of the waves discern;
Cast but a stone, or strike them with an oar,
And you shall flames within the deep explore;
Or scoop the stream phosphoric as you stand,
And the cold flames shall flash along your hand;
When, lost in wonder, you shall walk and gaze
On weeds that sparkle, and on waves that blaze.   110

The ocean too has winter-views serene,
When all you see through densest fog is seen;
When you can hear the fishers near at hand
Distinctly speak, yet see not where they stand;
Or sometimes them and not their boat discern,
Or half-conceal'd some figure at the stern;
The view's all bounded, and from side to side
Your utmost prospect but a few ells wide;

Boys who, on shore, to sea the pebble cast,
Will hear it strike against the viewless mast; 120
While the stern boatman growls his fierce disdain,
At whom he knows not, whom he threats in vain.
　'Tis pleasant then to view the nets float past,
Net after net till you have seen the last;
And as you wait till all beyond you slip,
A boat comes gliding from an anchor'd ship,
Breaking the silence with the dipping oar,
And their own tones, as labouring for the shore;
Those measured tones which with the scene agree,
And give a sadness to serenity. 130
　All scenes like these the tender maid should shun,
Nor to a misty beach in autumn run;
Much should she guard against the evening cold,
And her slight shape with fleecy warmth infold;
This she admits, but not with so much ease
Gives up the night-walk when th'attendants please;
Her have I seen, pale, vapour'd through the day,
With crowded parties at the midnight play;
Faint in the morn, no powers could she exert;
At night with Pam delighted and alert; 140
In a small shop she's raffled with a crowd,
Breathed the thick air, and cough'd and laugh'd aloud;
She who will tremble if her eye explore
"The smallest monstrous mouse that creeps on floor;"
Whom the kind doctor charged with shaking head,
At early hour to quit the beaux for bed:
She has, contemning fear, gone down the dance,
Till she perceived the rosy morn advance;
Then has she wonder'd, fainting o'er her tea,
Her drops and julep should so useless be: 150
Ah! sure her joys must ravish every sense,
Who buys a portion at such vast expense.
　Among those joys, 'tis one at eve to sail
On the broad river with a favourite gale;

When no rough waves upon the bosom ride,
But the keel cuts, nor rises on the tide;
Safe from the stream the nearer gunwale stands,
Where playful children trail their idle hands:
Or strive to catch long grassy leaves that float
On either side of the impeded boat;   160
What time the moon arising shows the mud,
A shining border to the silver flood:
When, by her dubious light, the meanest views,
Chalk, stones, and stakes, obtain the richest hues;
And when the cattle, as they gazing stand,
Seem nobler objects than when view'd from land:
Then anchor'd vessels in the way appear,
And sea-boys greet them as they pass – "What cheer?"
The sleeping shell-ducks at the sound arise,
And utter loud their unharmonious cries;   170
Fluttering they move their weedy beds among,
Or instant diving, hide their plumeless young.
    Along the wall, returning from the town,
The weary rustic homeward wanders down;
Who stops and gazes at such joyous crew,
And feels his envy rising at the view;
He the light speech and laugh indignant hears,
And feels more press'd by want, more vex'd by fears.
    Ah! go in peace, good fellow, to thine home,
Nor fancy these escape the general doom;   180
Gay as they seem, be sure with them are hearts
With sorrow tried; there's sadness in their parts:
If thou couldst see them when they think alone,
Mirth, music, friends, and these amusements gone;
Couldst thou discover every secret ill
That pains their spirit, or resists their will;
Couldst thou behold forsaken Love's distress,
Or Envy's pang at glory and success,
Or Beauty, conscious of the spoils of Time,
Or Guilt alarm'd when Memory shows the crime;   190

53

All that gives sorrow, terror, grief, and gloom;
Content would cheer thee trudging to thy home.
    There are, 'tis true, who lay their cares aside,
And bid some hours in calm enjoyment glide;
Perchance some fair-one to the sober night
Adds (by the sweetness of her song) delight;
And, as the music on the water floats,
Some bolder shore returns the soften'd notes;
Then, youth, beware, for all around conspire
To banish caution and to wake desire;   200
The day's amusement, feasting, beauty, wine,
These accents sweet and this soft hour combine,
When most unguarded, then to win that heart of thine:
But see, they land! the fond enchantment flies,
And in its place life's common views arise.
    Sometimes a party, row'd from town, will land
On a small islet form'd of shelly sand,
Left by the water when the tides are low,
But which the floods in their return o'erflow:
There will they anchor, pleased awhile to view   210
The watery waste, a prospect wild and new;
The now receding billows give them space,
On either side the growing shores to pace;
And then returning, they contract the scene,
Till small and smaller grows the walk between;
As sea to sea approaches, shore to shores,
Till the next ebb the sandy isle restores.
    Then what alarm! what danger and dismay,
If all their trust, their boat should drift away;
And once it happen'd – gay the friends advanced,   220
They walk'd, they ran, they play'd, they sang, they danced;
The urns were boiling, and the cups went round,
And not a grave or thoughtful face was found;
On the bright sand they trod with nimble feet,
Dry shelly sand that made the summer-seat;
The wondering mews flew fluttering o'er the head,

And waves ran softly up their shining bed.
   Some form'd a party from the rest to stray,
Pleased to collect the trifles in their way;
These to behold they call their friends around,   230
No friends can hear, or hear another sound;
Alarm'd, they hasten, yet perceive not why,
But catch the fear that quickens as they fly.
   For lo! a lady sage, who paced the sand
With her fair children, one in either hand,
Intent on home, had turn'd, and saw the boat
Slipp'd from her moorings, and now far afloat;
She gazed, she trembled, and though faint her call,
It seem'd, like thunder, to confound them all.
Their sailor-guides, the boatman and his mate,   240
Had drank, and slept regardless of their state;
"Awake!" they cried aloud; "Alarm the shore!
"Shout all, or never shall we reach it more!"
Alas! no shout the distant land can reach,
Nor eye behold them from the foggy beach:
Again they join in one loud powerful cry,
Then cease, and eager listen for reply;
None came – the rising wind blew sadly by:
They shout once more, and then they turn aside,
To see how quickly flow'd the coming tide;   250
Between each cry they find the waters steal
On their strange prison, and new horrors feel;
Foot after foot on the contracted ground
The billows fall, and dreadful is the sound;
Less and yet less the sinking isle became,
And there was wailing, weeping, wrath, and blame.
   Had one been there, with spirit strong and high,
Who could observe, as he prepared to die,
He might have seen of hearts the varying kind,
And traced the movement of each different mind: 260
He might have seen, that not the gentle maid
Was more than stern and haughty man afraid;

Such, calmly grieving, will their fears suppress,
And silent prayers to Mercy's throne address;
While fiercer minds, impatient, angry, loud,
Force their vain grief on the reluctant crowd:
The party's patron, sorely sighing, cried,
"Why would you urge me? I at first denied."
Fiercely they answer'd, "Why will you complain,
"Who saw no danger, or was warn'd in vain?"   270
A few essay'd the troubled soul to calm,
But dread prevail'd, and anguish and alarm.

   Now rose the water through the lessening sand,
And they seem'd sinking while they yet could stand;
The sun went down, they look'd from side to side,
Nor aught except the gathering sea descried;
Dark and more dark, more wet, more cold it grew,
And the most lively bade to hope adieu;
Children, by love then lifted from the seas,
Felt not the waters at the parents' knees,   280
But wept aloud; the wind increased the sound,
And the cold billows as they broke around.

   "Once more, yet once again, with all our strength,
"Cry to the land – we may be heard at length."
Vain hope, if yet unseen! but hark! an oar,
That sound of bliss! comes dashing to their shore;
Still, still the water rises, "Haste!" they cry,
"Oh! hurry, seamen; in delay we die:"
(Seamen were these, who in their ship perceived
The drifted boat, and thus her crew relieved.)   290
And now the keel just cuts the cover'd sand,
Now to the gunwale stretches every hand:
With trembling pleasure all confused embark,
And kiss the tackling of their welcome ark;
While the most giddy, as they reach the shore,
Think of their danger, and their God adore.

The Poor and Their Dwellings

Yes! we've our Borough-vices, and I know
How far they spread, how rapidly they grow;
Yet think not virtue quits the busy place,
Nor charity, the virtues' crown and grace.
    "Our poor, how feed we?" – To the most we give
A weekly dole, and at their homes they live; –
Others together dwell, – but when they come
To the low roof, they see a kind of home,
A social people whom they've ever known,
With their own thoughts and manners like their own.   10
    At her old house, her dress, her air the same,
I see mine ancient letter-loving dame:
"Learning, my child," said she, "shall fame command;
"Learning is better worth than house or land –
"For houses perish, lands are gone and spent;
"In learning then excel, for that's most excellent."
    "And what her learning?" – 'Tis with awe to look
In every verse throughout one sacred book;
From this her joy, her hope, her peace is sought:
This she has learn'd, and she is nobly taught.   20
    If aught of mine have gain'd the public ear;
If Rutland deigns these humble Tales to hear;
If critics pardon, what my friends approved;
Can I mine ancient widow pass unmoved?
Shall I not think what pains the matron took,
When first I trembled o'er the gilded book?
How she, all patient, both at eve and morn,
Her needle pointed at the guarding horn;
And how she soothed me, when, with study sad,
I labour'd on to reach the final zad?   30
Shall I not grateful still the dame survey,
And ask the muse the poet's debt to pay?
    Nor I alone, who hold a trifler's pen,

57

But half our bench of wealthy, weighty men,
Who rule our Borough, who enforce our laws;
They own the matron as the leading cause,
And feel the pleasing debt, and pay the just applause:
To her own house is borne the week's supply;
There she in credit lives, there hopes in peace to die.

With her a harmless idiot we behold, 40
Who hoards up silver shells for shining gold;
These he preserves, with unremitted care,
To buy a seat, and reign the Borough's mayor:
Alas! – who could th'ambitious changeling tell,
That what he sought our rulers dared to sell?

Near these a sailor, in that hut of thatch
(A fish-boat's cabin is its nearest match),
Dwells, and the dungeon is to him a seat,
Large as he wishes – in his view complete:
A lockless coffer and a lidless hutch 50
That holds his stores, have room for twice as much:
His one spare shirt, long glass, and iron box,
Lie all in view; no need has he for locks:
Here he abides, and, as our strangers pass,
He shows the shipping, he presents the glass;
He makes (unask'd) their ports and business known,
And (kindly heard) turns quickly to his own,
Of noble captains, heroes every one, –
You might as soon have made the steeple run:
And then his messmates, if you're pleased to stay, 60
He'll one by one the gallant souls display,
And as the story verges to an end,
He'll wind from deed to deed, from friend to friend;
He'll speak of those long lost, the brave of old,
As princes gen'rous and as heroes bold;
Then will his feelings rise, till you may trace
Gloom, like a cloud, frown o'er his manly face, –
And then a tear or two, which sting his pride;
These he will dash indignantly aside,

And splice his tale; – now take him from his cot,   70
And for some cleaner berth exchange his lot,
How will he all that cruel aid deplore?
His heart will break, and he will fight no more.

Here is the poor old merchant: he declined,
And, as they say, is not in perfect mind;
In his poor house, with one poor maiden friend,
Quiet he paces to his journey's end.

Rich in his youth, he traded and he fail'd;
Again he tried, again his fate prevail'd;
His spirits low and his exertions small,   80
He fell perforce, he seem'd decreed to fall:
Like the gay knight, unapt to rise was he,
But downward sank with sad alacrity.
A borough-place we gain'd him – in disgrace
For gross neglect, he quickly lost the place;
But still he kept a kind of sullen pride,
Striving his wants to hinder or to hide:
At length, compell'd by very need, in grief
He wrote a proud petition for relief.

"He did suppose a fall, like his, would prove   90
"Of force to wake their sympathy and love;
"Would make them feel the changes all may know,
"And stir them up a new regard to show."

His suit was granted; – to an ancient maid,
Relieved herself, relief for him was paid:
Here they together (meet companions) dwell,
And dismal tales of man's misfortunes tell:
"'Twas not a world for them, God help them! they
"Could not deceive, nor flatter, nor betray;
"But there's a happy change, a scene to come,   100
"And they, God help them! shall be soon at home."

If these no pleasures nor enjoyments gain,
Still none their spirits nor their speech restrain;
They sigh at ease, 'mid comforts they complain.
The poor will grieve, the poor will weep and sigh,

Both when they know, and when they know not why;
But we our bounty with such care bestow,
That cause for grieving they shall seldom know.
　　Your plan I love not; – with a number you
Have placed your poor, your pitiable few;　　　　　　　　110
There, in one house, throughout their lives to be,
The pauper-palace which they hate to see:
That giant-building, that high-bounding wall,
Those bare-worn walks, that lofty thund'ring hall!
That large loud clock, which tolls each dreaded hour,
Those gates and locks, and all those signs of power:
It is a prison, with a milder name,
Which few inhabit without dread or shame.
　　Be it agreed – the poor who hither come
Partake of plenty, seldom found at home;　　　　　　　　120
That airy rooms and decent beds are meant
To give the poor by day, by night, content;
That none are frighten'd, once admitted here,
By the stern looks of lordly overseer:
Grant that the guardians of the place attend,
And ready ear to each petition lend;
That they desire the grieving poor to show
What ills they feel, what partial acts they know,
Not without promise, nay desire to heal
Each wrong they suffer and each wo they feel.　　　　　　130
　　Alas! their sorrows in their bosoms dwell;
They've much to suffer, but have nought to tell;
They have no evil in the place to state,
And dare not say, it is the house they hate:
They own there's granted all such place can give,
But live repining, for 'tis there they live.
　　Grandsires are there, who now no more must see,
No more must nurse upon the trembling knee
The lost loved daughter's infant progeny:
Like death's dread mansion, this allows not place　　　　140
For joyful meetings of a kindred race.

Is not the matron there, to whom the son
Was wont at each declining day to run;
He (when his toil was over) gave delight,
By lifting up the latch, and one "good night?"
Yes, she is here; but nightly to her door
The son, still lab'ring, can return no more.
Widows are here, who in their huts were left,
Of husbands, children, plenty, ease bereft;
Yet all that grief within the humble shed   150
Was soften'd, soften'd in the humble bed:
But here, in all its force, remains the grief,
And not one soft'ning object for relief.

Who can, when here, the social neighbour meet?
Who learn the story current in the street?
Who to the long-known intimate impart
Facts they have learn'd or feelings of the heart? –
They talk indeed, but who can choose a friend,
Or seek companions at their journey's end?

Here are not those whom they, when infants, knew;   160
Who, with like fortune, up to manhood grew;
Who, with like troubles, at old age arrived;
Who, like themselves, the joy of life survived;
Whom time and custom so familiar made,
That looks the meaning in the mind convey'd:
But here to strangers, words nor looks impart
The various movements of the suffering heart;
Nor will that heart with those alliance own,
To whom its views and hopes are all unknown.

What, if no grievous fears their lives annoy,   170
Is it not worse no prospects to enjoy?
'Tis cheerless living in such bounded view,
With nothing dreadful, but with nothing new;
Nothing to bring them joy, to make them weep, –
The day itself is, like the night, asleep:
Or on the sameness if a break be made,
'Tis by some pauper to his grave convey'd;

61

By smuggled news from neighb'ring village told,
News never true, or truth a twelvemonth old;
By some new inmate doom'd with them to dwell,   180
Or justice come to see that all goes well;
Or change of room, or hour of leave to crawl
On the black footway winding with the wall,
Till the stern bell forbids, or master's sterner call.
    Here too the mother sees her children train'd,
Her voice excluded and her feelings pain'd:
Who govern here, by general rules must move,
Where ruthless custom rends the bond of love.
Nations we know have nature's law transgress'd,
And snatch'd the infant from the parent's breast;   190
But still for public good the boy was train'd,
The mother suffer'd, but the matron gain'd:
Here nature's outrage serves no cause to aid;
The ill is felt, but not the Spartan made.
    Then too I own, it grieves me to behold
Those ever virtuous, helpless now and old,
By all for care and industry approved,
For truth respected, and for temper loved;
And who, by sickness and misfortune tried,
Gave want its worth and poverty its pride: 200
I own it grieves me to behold them sent
From their old home; 'tis pain, 'tis punishment,
To leave each scene familiar, every face,
For a new people and a stranger race;
For those who, sunk in sloth and dead to shame,
From scenes of guilt with daring spirits came;
Men, just and guileless, at such manners start,
And bless their God that time has fenced their heart,
Confirm'd their virtue, and expell'd the fear
Of vice in minds so simple and sincere.   210
    Here the good pauper, losing all the praise
By worthy deeds acquired in better days,
Breathes a few months, then, to his chamber led,

Expires, while strangers prattle round his bed.
   The grateful hunter, when his horse is old,
Wills not the useless favourite to be sold;
He knows his former worth, and gives him place
In some fair pasture, till he runs his race:
But has the labourer, has the seaman done
Less worthy service, though not dealt to one?   220
Shall we not then contribute to their ease,
In their old haunts, where ancient objects please?
That, till their sight shall fail them, they may trace
The well-known prospect and the long-loved face.
   The noble oak, in distant ages seen,
With far-stretch'd boughs and foliage fresh and green,
Though now its bare and forky branches show
How much it lacks the vital warmth below,
The stately ruin yet our wonder gains,
Nay, moves our pity, without thought of pains: 230
Much more shall real wants and cares of age
Our gentler passions in their cause engage; –
Drooping and burthen'd with a weight of years,
What venerable ruin man appears!
How worthy pity, love, respect, and grief –
He claims protection – he compels relief; –
And shall we send him from our view, to brave
The storms abroad, whom we at home might save,
And let a stranger dig our ancient brother's grave?
No! – we will shield him from the storm he fears,   240
And when he falls, embalm him with our tears.
                         *

   Farewell to these; but all our poor to know,
Let's seek the winding lane, the narrow row,
Suburban prospects, where the traveller stops
To see the sloping tenement on props,
With building yards immix'd, and humble sheds and shops;
Where the Cross-Keys and Plumber's-Arms invite
Laborious men to taste their coarse delight;

63

Where the low porches, stretching from the door,
Gave some distinction in the days of yore, 250
Yet now neglected, more offend the eye,
By gloom and ruin, than the cottage by:
Places like these the noblest town endures,
The gayest palace has its sinks and sewers.

Here is no pavement, no inviting shop,
To give us shelter when compell'd to stop;
But plashy puddles stand along the way,
Fill'd by the rain of one tempestuous day;
And these so closely to the buildings run,
That you must ford them, for you cannot shun; 260
Though here and there convenient bricks are laid,
And door-side heaps afford their dubious aid.

Lo! yonder shed; observe its garden-ground,
With the low paling, form'd of wreck, around:
There dwells a fisher; if you view his boat,
With bed and barrel – 'tis his house afloat;
Look at his house, where ropes, nets, blocks, abound,
Tar, pitch, and oakum – 'tis his boat aground:
That space enclosed, but little he regards,
Spread o'er with relics of masts, sails, and yards: 270
Fish by the wall, on spit of elder, rest,
Of all his food, the cheapest and the best,
By his own labour caught, for his own hunger dress'd.

Here our reformers come not; none object
To paths polluted, or upbraid neglect;
None care that ashy heaps at doors are cast,
That coal-dust flies along the blinding blast:
None heed the stagnant pools on either side,
Where new-launch'd ships of infant sailors ride:
Rodneys in rags here British valour boast, 280
And lisping Nelsons fright the Gallic coast.
They fix the rudder, set the swelling sail,
They point the bowsprit, and they blow the gale:
True to her port, the frigate scuds away,

64

And o'er that frowning ocean finds her bay:
Her owner rigg'd her, and he knows her worth,
And sees her, fearless, gunwale-deep go forth;
Dreadless he views his sea, by breezes curl'd,
When inch-high billows vex the watery world.
    There, fed by food they love, to rankest size,   290
Around the dwellings docks and wormwood rise;
Here the strong mallow strikes her slimy root,
Here the dull night-shade hangs her deadly fruit;
On hills of dust the henbane's faded green,
And pencil'd flower of sickly scent is seen;
At the wall's base the fiery nettle springs,
With fruit globose and fierce with poison'd stings;
Above (the growth of many a year) is spread
The yellow level of the stone-crop's bed;
In every chink delights the fern to grow,   300
With glossy leaf and tawny bloom below:
These, with our sea-weeds, rolling up and down,
Form the contracted Flora of the town.
    Say, wilt thou more of scenes so sordid know?
Then will I lead thee down the dusty row;
By the warm alley and the long close lane, –
There mark the fractured door and paper'd pane,
Where flags the noon-tide air, and, as we pass,
We fear to breathe the putrefying mass:
But fearless yonder matron; she disdains   310
To sigh for zephyrs from ambrosial plains;
But mends her meshes torn, and pours her lay
All in the stifling fervour of the day.
    Her naked children round the alley run,
And roll'd in dust, are bronzed beneath the sun;
Or gambol round the dame, who, loosely dress'd,
Woos the coy breeze, to fan the open breast:
She, once a handmaid, strove by decent art
To charm her sailor's eye and touch his heart;
Her bosom then was veil'd in kerchief clean,   320

And fancy left to form the charms unseen.

   But when a wife, she lost her former care,
Nor thought on charms, nor time for dress could spare;
Careless she found her friends who dwelt beside,
No rival beauty kept alive her pride:
Still in her bosom virtue keeps her place,
But decency is gone, the virtues' guard and grace.

   See that long boarded building! – By these stairs
Each humble tenant to that home repairs –
By one large window lighted – it was made   330
For some bold project, some design in trade:
This fail'd, – and one, a humorist in his way,
(Ill was the humour), bought it in decay;
Nor will he sell, repair, or take it down;
'Tis his, – what cares he for the talk of town?
"No! he will let it to the poor; – a home
"Where he delights to see the creatures come:"
"They may be thieves;" – "Well, so are richer men;"
"Or idlers, cheats, or prostitutes:" – "What then?"
"Outcasts pursued by justice, vile and base;" –   340
"They need the more his pity and the place:"
Convert to system his vain mind has built,
He gives asylum to deceit and guilt.

   In this vast room, each place by habit fix'd,
Are sexes, families, and ages mix'd, –
To union forced by crime, by fear, by need,
And all in morals and in modes agreed;
Some ruin'd men, who from mankind remove;
Some ruin'd females, who yet talk of love;
And some grown old in idleness – the prey   350
To vicious spleen, still railing through the day;
And need and misery, vice and danger bind
In sad alliance each degraded mind.

   That window view! – oil'd paper and old glass
Stain the strong rays which, though impeded, pass,
And give a dusty warmth to that huge room,

The conquer'd sunshine's melancholy gloom;
When all those western rays, without so bright,
Within become a ghastly glimmering light,
As pale and faint upon the floor they fall,   360
Or feebly gleam on the opposing wall:
That floor, once oak, now pieced with fir unplaned,
Or, where not pieced, in places bored and stain'd;
That wall once whiten'd, now an odious sight,
Stain'd with all hues, except its ancient white;
The only door is fasten'd by a pin,
Or stubborn bar, that none may hurry in:
For this poor room, like rooms of greater pride,
At times contains what prudent men would hide.

    Where'er the floor allows an even space,   370
Chalking and marks of various games have place;
Boys without foresight, pleased in halters swing;
On a fix'd hook men cast a flying ring;
While gin and snuff their female neighbours share,
And the black beverage in the fractured ware.

    On swinging shelf are things incongruous stored, –
Scraps of their food, – the cards and cribbage-board, –
With pipes and pouches; while on peg below,
Hang a lost member's fiddle and its bow:
That still reminds them how he'd dance and play,   380
Ere sent untimely to the convicts' bay.

    Here by a curtain, by a blanket there,
Are various beds conceal'd, but none with care;
Where some by day and some by night, as best
Suit their employments, seek uncertain rest;
The drowsy children at their pleasure creep
To the known crib, and there securely sleep.

    Each end contains a grate, and these beside
Are hung utensils for their boil'd and fried –
All used at any hour, by night, by day,   390
As suit the purse, the person, or the prey.

    Above the fire, the mantel-shelf contains

Of china-ware some poor unmatch'd remains;
There many a tea-cup's gaudy fragment stands,
All placed by vanity's unwearied hands;
For here she lives, e'en here she looks about,
To find some small consoling objects out:
Nor heed these Spartan dames their house, nor sit
'Mid cares domestic, – they nor sew nor knit;
But of their fate discourse, their ways, their wars,   400
With arm'd authorities, their 'scapes and scars:
These lead to present evils, and a cup,
If fortune grant it, winds description up.

   High hung at either end, and next the wall,
Two ancient mirrors show the forms of all,
In all their force; – these aid them in their dress,
But with the good, the evils too express,
Doubling each look of care, each token of distress.

LETTER XIX
The Parish-Clerk

With our late vicar, and his age the same,
His clerk, hight Jachin, to his office came;
The like slow speech was his, the like tall slender frame:
But Jachin was the gravest man on ground,
And heard his master's jokes with look profound;
For worldly wealth this man of letters sigh'd,
And had a sprinkling of the spirit's pride:
But he was sober, chaste, devout, and just,
One whom his neighbours could believe and trust:
Of none suspected, neither man nor maid   10
By him were wrong'd, or were of him afraid.

   There was indeed a frown, a trick of state
In Jachin; – formal was his air and gait;
But if he seemed more solemn and less kind

Than some light men to light affairs confined,
Still 'twas allow'd that he should so behave
As in high seat, and be severely grave.
   This book-taught man, to man's first foe profess'd
Defiance stern, and hate that knew not rest;
He held that Satan, since the world began,   20
In every act, had strife with every man;
That never evil deed on earth was done,
But of the acting parties he was one;
The flattering guide to make ill prospects clear;
To smooth rough ways the constant pioneer;
The ever-tempting, soothing, softening power,
Ready to cheat, seduce, deceive, devour.
   "Me has the sly seducer oft withstood,"
Said pious Jachin, – "but he gets no good;
"I pass the house where swings the tempting sign,   30
"And pointing, tell him, 'Satan, that is thine:'
"I pass the damsels pacing down the street,
"And look more grave and solemn when we meet;
"Nor doth it irk me to rebuke their smiles,
"Their wanton ambling and their watchful wiles:
"Nay, like the good John Bunyan, when I view
"Those forms, I'm angry at the ills they do;
"That I could pinch and spoil, in sin's despite,
"Beauties! which frail and evil thoughts excite.
   "At feasts and banquets seldom am I found,   40
"And (save at church) abhor a tuneful sound;
"To plays and shows I run not to and fro,
"And where my master goes forbear to go."
   No wonder Satan took the thing amiss,
To be opposed by such a man as this –
A man so grave, important, cautious, wise,
Who dared not trust his feeling or his eyes;
No wonder he should lurk and lie in wait,
Should fit his hooks and ponder on his bait,
Should on his movements keep a watchful eye;   50

69

For he pursued a fish who led the fry.
     With his own peace our clerk was not content,
He tried, good man! to make his friends repent.
     "Nay, nay, my friends, from inns and taverns fly;
"You may suppress your thirst, but not supply:
"A foolish proverb says, 'the devil's at home;'
"But he is there, and tempts in every room:
"Men feel, they know not why, such places please;
"His are the spells – they're idleness and ease;
"Magic of fatal kind he throws around,   60
"Where care is banish'd but the heart is bound.
     "Think not of beauty; when a maid you meet,
"Turn from her view and step across the street;
"Dread all the sex: their looks create a charm,
"A smile should fright you and a word alarm:
"E'en I myself, with all my watchful care,
"Have for an instant felt th'insidious snare,
"And caught my sinful eyes at th'endangering stare;
"Till I was forced to smite my bounding breast
"With forceful blow and bid the bold-one rest.   70
     "Go not with crowds when they to pleasure run,
"But public joy in private safety shun:
"When bells, diverted from their true intent,
"Ring loud for some deluded mortal sent
"To hear or make long speech in parliament;
"What time the many, that unruly beast,
"Roars its rough joy and shares the final feast:
"Then heed my counsel, shut thine ears and eyes;
"A few will hear me – for the few are wise."
     Not Satan's friends, nor Satan's self could bear   80
The cautious man who took of souls such care;
An interloper, – one who, out of place,
Had volunteer'd upon the side of grace:
There was his master ready once a week
To give advice; what further need he seek?
"Amen, so be it:" – what had he to do

With more than this? – 'twas insolent and new;
And some determined on a way to see
How frail he was, that so it might not be.
  First they essay'd to tempt our saint to sin,   90
By points of doctrine argued at an inn;
Where he might warmly reason, deeply drink,
Then lose all power to argue and to think.
  In vain they tried; he took the question up,
Clear'd every doubt, and barely touch'd the cup:
By many a text he proved his doctrine sound,
And look'd in triumph on the tempters round.
  Next 'twas their care an artful lass to find,
Who might consult him, as perplex'd in mind;
She they conceived might put her case with fears,   100
With tender tremblings and seducing tears;
She might such charms of various kind display,
That he would feel their force and melt away:
For why of nymphs such caution and such dread,
Unless he felt and fear'd to be misled?
  She came, she spake: he calmly heard her case,
And plainly told her 'twas a want of grace;
Bade her "such fancies and affections check,
"And wear a thicker muslin on her neck."
Abased, his human foes the combat fled,   110
And the stern clerk yet higher held his head.
They were indeed a weak, impatient set,
But their shrewd prompter had his engines yet;
Had various means to make a mortal trip,
Who shunn'd a flowing bowl and rosy lip;
And knew a thousand ways his heart to move,
Who flies from banquets and who laughs at love.
  Thus far the playful Muse has lent her aid,
But now departs, of graver theme afraid;
Her may we seek in more appropriate time, –   120
There is no jesting with distress and crime.
  Our worthy clerk had now arrived at fame,

Such as but few in his degree might claim;
But he was poor, and wanted not the sense
That lowly rates the praise without the pence:
He saw the common herd with reverence treat
The weakest burgess whom they chanced to meet;
While few respected his exalted views,
And all beheld his doublet and his shoes:
None, when they meet, would to his parts allow   130
(Save his poor boys) a hearing or a bow:
To this false judgment of the vulgar mind,
He was not fully, as a saint, resign'd;
He found it much his jealous soul affect,
To fear derision and to find neglect.

    The year was bad, the christening-fees were small,
The weddings few, the parties paupers all:
Desire of gain with fear of want combined,
Raised sad commotion in his wounded mind;
Wealth was in all his thoughts, his views, his dreams, 140
And prompted base desires and baseless schemes.

    Alas! how often erring mortals keep
The strongest watch against the foes who sleep;
While the more wakeful, bold and artful foe
Is suffer'd guardless and unmark'd to go.

    Once in a month the sacramental bread
Our clerk with wine upon the table spread;
The custom this, that, as the vicar reads,
He for our off'rings round the church proceeds:
Tall spacious seats the wealthier people hid,   150
And none had view of what his neighbour did;
Laid on the box and mingled when they fell,
Who should the worth of each oblation tell?
Now as poor Jachin took the usual round,
And saw the alms and heard the metal sound,
He had a thought; – at first it was no more
Than – "these have cash and give it to the poor:"
A second thought from this to work began –

"And can they give it to a poorer man?"
Proceeding thus, – "My merit could they know,   160
"And knew my need, how freely they'd bestow;
"But though they know not, these remain the same;
"And are a strong, although a secret claim:
"To me, alas! the want and worth are known,
Why then, in fact, 'tis but to take my own."
    Thought after thought pour'd in, a tempting train, –
"Suppose it done, – who is it could complain?
"How could the poor? for they such trifles share,
"As add no comfort, as suppress no care;
"But many a pittance makes a worthy heap, –   170
"What says the law? that silence puts to sleep: –
"Nought then forbids, the danger could we shun,
"And sure the business may be safely done.
    "But am I earnest? – earnest? No. – I say,
"If such my mind, that I could plan a way;
"Let me reflect; – I've not allowed me time
"To purse the pieces, and if dropp'd they'd chime:"
Fertile is evil in the soul of man, –
He paused, – said Jachin, "They may drop on bran.
"Why then 'tis safe and (all consider'd) just,   180
"The poor receive it, – 'tis no breach of trust:
"The old and widows may their trifles miss,
"There must be evil in a good like this:
"But I'll be kind – the sick I'll visit twice,
"When now but once, and freely give advice.
"Yet let me think again:" – Again he tried,
For stronger reasons on his passion's side,
And quickly these were found, yet slowly he complied.
    The morning came: the common service done, –
Shut every door, – the solemn rite begun, –   190
And, as the priest the sacred sayings read,
The clerk went forward, trembling as he tread;
O'er the tall pew he held the box, and heard
The offer'd piece, rejoicing as he fear'd:

Just by the pillar, as he cautious tripp'd,
And turn'd the aile, he then a portion slipp'd
From the full store, and to the pocket sent,
But held a moment – and then down it went.
　　The priest read on, on walk'd the man afraid,
Till a gold offering in the plate was laid; 200
Trembling he took it, for a moment stopp'd,
Then down it fell, and sounded as it dropp'd;
Amazed he started, for th'affrighted man,
Lost and bewilder'd, thought not of the bran;
But all were silent, all on things intent
Of high concern, none ear to money lent;
So on he walk'd, more cautious than before,
And gain'd the purposed sum and one piece more.
　　Practice makes perfect; – when the month came round,
He dropp'd the cash, nor listen'd for a sound; 210
But yet, when last of all th'assembled flock,
He ate and drank, – it gave th'electric shock:
Oft was he forced his reasons to repeat,
Ere he could kneel in quiet at his seat;
But custom soothed him – ere a single year
All this was done without restraint or fear:
Cool and collected, easy and composed,
He was correct till all the service closed;
Then to his home, without a groan or sigh,
Gravely he went, and laid his treasure by. 220
　　Want will complain: some widows had express'd
A doubt if they were favour'd like the rest;
The rest described with like regret their dole,
And thus from parts they reason'd to the whole;
When all agreed some evil must be done,
Or rich men's hearts grew harder than a stone.
　　Our easy vicar cut the matter short;
He would not listen to such vile report.
　　All were not thus – there govern'd in that year
A stern stout churl, an angry overseer; 230

A tyrant fond of power, loud, lewd, and most severe:
Him the mild vicar, him the graver clerk,
Advised, reproved, but nothing would he mark,
Save the disgrace, "and that, my friends," said he,
"Will I avenge, whenever time may be."
And now, alas! 'twas time; – from man to man
Doubt and alarm and shrewd suspicions ran.

    With angry spirit and with sly intent,
This parish-ruler to the altar went;
A private mark he fix'd on shillings three,   240
And but one mark could in the money see;
Besides, in peering round, he chanced to note
A sprinkling slight on Jachin's Sunday-coat:
All doubt was over: – when the flock were bless'd,
In wrath he rose, and thus his mind express'd.

    "Foul deeds are here!" and saying this, he took
The clerk, whose conscience, in her cold-fit, shook:
His pocket then was emptied on the place;
All saw his guilt; all witness'd his disgrace:
He fell, he fainted, not a groan, a look,   250
Escaped the culprit; 'twas a final stroke –
A death-wound never to be heal'd – a fall
That all had witness'd, and amazed were all.

    As he recover'd, to his mind it came,
"I owe to Satan this disgrace and shame:"
All the seduction now appear'd in view;
"Let me withdraw," he said, and he withdrew;
No one withheld him, all in union cried,
E'en the avenger, – "We are satisfied:"
For what has death in any form to give,   260
Equal to that man's terrors, if he live?

    He lived in freedom, but he hourly saw
How much more fatal justice is than law;
He saw another in his office reign,
And his mild master treat him with disdain;
He saw that all men shunn'd him, some reviled,

The harsh pass'd frowning, and the simple smiled;
The town maintain'd him, but with some reproof,
"And clerks and scholars proudly kept aloof."
    In each lone place, dejected and dismay'd,   270
Shrinking from view, his wasting form he laid;
Or to the restless sea and roaring wind
Gave the strong yearnings of a ruin'd mind:
On the broad beach, the silent summer-day,
Stretch'd on some wreck, he wore his life away;
Or where the river mingles with the sea,
Or on the mud-bank by the elder-tree,
Or by the bounding marsh-dyke, there was he:
And when unable to forsake the town,
In the blind courts he sate desponding down –   280
Always alone; then feebly would he crawl
The church-way walk, and lean upon the wall:
Too ill for this, he lay beside the door,
Compell'd to hear the reasoning of the poor:
He look'd so pale, so weak, the pitying crowd
Their firm belief of his repentance vow'd;
They saw him then so ghastly and so thin,
That they exclaimed, "Is this the work of sin?"
    "Yes," in his better moments, he replied,
"Of sinful avarice and the spirit's pride; –   290
"While yet untempted, I was safe and well;
"Temptation came; I reason'd, and I fell:
"To be man's guide and glory I design'd,
"A rare example for our sinful kind;
"But now my weakness and my guilt I see,
"And am a warning – man, be warn'd by me!"
    He said, and saw no more the human face;
To a lone loft he went, his dying place,
And, as the vicar of his state inquired,
Turn'd to the wall and silently expired!   300

Peter Grimes

Old Peter Grimes made fishing his employ,
His wife he cabin'd with him and his boy,
And seem'd that life laborious to enjoy:
To town came quiet Peter with his fish,
And had of all a civil word and wish.
He left his trade upon the sabbath-day,
And took young Peter in his hand to pray:
But soon the stubborn boy from care broke loose,
At first refused, then added his abuse:
His father's love he scorn'd, his power defied,   10
But being drunk, wept sorely when he died.
    Yes! then he wept, and to his mind there came
Much of his conduct, and he felt the shame, –
How he had oft the good old man reviled,
And never paid the duty of a child;
How, when the father in his Bible read,
He in contempt and anger left the shed:
"It is the word of life," the parent cried;
– "This is the life itself," the boy replied;
And while old Peter in amazement stood,   20
Gave the hot spirit to his boiling blood: –
How he, with oath and furious speech, began
To prove his freedom and assert the man;
And when the parent check'd his impious rage,
How he had cursed the tyranny of age, –
Nay, once had dealt the sacrilegious blow
On his bare head, and laid his parent low;
The father groan'd – "If thou art old," said he,
"And hast a son – thou wilt remember me:
"Thy mother left me in a happy time,   30
"Thou kill'dst not her – Heav'n spares the double crime."
    On an inn-settle, in his maudlin grief,
This he revolved, and drank for his relief.

77

Now lived the youth in freedom, but debarr'd
From constant pleasure, and he thought it hard;
Hard that he could not every wish obey,
But must awhile relinquish ale and play;
Hard! that he could not to his cards attend,
But must acquire the money he would spend.
  With greedy eye he look'd on all he saw,   40
He knew not justice, and he laugh'd at law;
On all he mark'd he stretch'd his ready hand;
He fish'd by water, and he filch'd by land:
Oft in the night has Peter dropp'd his oar,
Fled from his boat and sought for prey on shore;
Oft up the hedge-row glided, on his back
Bearing the orchard's produce in a sack,
Or farm-yard load, tugg'd fiercely from the stack;
And as these wrongs to greater numbers rose,
The more he look'd on all men as his foes.   50
  He built a mud-wall'd hovel, where he kept
His various wealth, and there he oft-times slept;
But no success could please his cruel soul,
He wish'd for one to trouble and control;
He wanted some obedient boy to stand
And bear the blow of his outrageous hand;
And hoped to find in some propitious hour
A feeling creature subject to his power.
  Peter had heard there were in London then, –
Still have they being! – workhouse-clearing men,   60
Who, undisturb'd by feelings just or kind,
Would parish-boys to needy tradesmen bind:
They in their want a trifling sum would take,
And toiling slaves of piteous orphans make.
  Such Peter sought, and when a lad was found,
The sum was dealt him, and the slave was bound.
Some few in town observed in Peter's trap
A boy, with jacket blue and woollen cap;
But none inquired how Peter used the rope,

Or what the bruise, that made the stripling stoop;   70
None could the ridges on his back behold,
None sought him shiv'ring in the winter's cold;
None put the question, – "Peter, dost thou give
"The boy his food? – What, man! the lad must live:
"Consider, Peter, let the child have bread,
"He'll serve thee better if he's stroked and fed."
None reason'd thus – and some, on hearing cries,
Said calmly, "Grimes is at his exercise."
    Pinn'd, beaten, cold, pinch'd, threaten'd, and abused –
His efforts punish'd and his food refused, –   80
Awake tormented, – soon aroused from sleep, –
Struck if he wept, and yet compell'd to weep,
The trembling boy dropp'd down and strove to pray,
Received a blow, and trembling turn'd away,
Or sobb'd and hid his piteous face; – while he,
The savage master, grinn'd in horrid glee:
He'd now the power he ever loved to show,
A feeling being subject to his blow.
    Thus lived the lad, in hunger, peril, pain,
His tears despised, his supplications vain: 90
Compell'd by fear to lie, by need to steal,
His bed uneasy and unbless'd his meal,
For three sad years the boy his tortures bore,
And then his pains and trials were no more.
    "How died he, Peter?" when the people said,
He growl'd – "I found him lifeless in his bed;"
Then tried for softer tone, and sigh'd, "Poor Sam is dead."
Yet murmurs were there, and some questions ask'd, –
How he was fed, how punish'd, and how task'd?
Much they suspected, but they little proved,   100
And Peter pass'd untroubled and unmoved.
    Another boy with equal ease was found,
The money granted, and the victim bound;
And what his fate? – One night it chanced he fell
From the boat's mast and perish'd in her well,

Where fish were living kept, and where the boy
(So reason'd men) could not himself destroy: –
      "Yes! so it was," said Peter, "in his play,
"(For he was idle both by night and day,)
"He climb'd the main-mast and then fell below;" –   110
Then show'd his corpse and pointed to the blow:
"What said the jury?" – they were long in doubt,
But sturdy Peter faced the matter out:
So they dismiss'd him, saying at the time,
"Keep fast your hatchway when you've boys who climb."
This hit the conscience, and he colour'd more
Than for the closest questions put before.
      Thus all his fears the verdict set aside,
And at the slave-shop Peter still applied.
      Then came a boy, of manners soft and mild, –   120
Our seamen's wives with grief beheld the child;
All thought (the poor themselves) that he was one
Of gentle blood, some noble sinner's son,
Who had, belike, deceived some humble maid,
Whom he had first seduced and then betray'd: –
However this, he seem'd a gracious lad,
In grief submissive and with patience sad.
      Passive he labour'd, till his slender frame
Bent with his loads, and he at length was lame:
Strange that a frame so weak could bear so long   130
The grossest insult and the foulest wrong;
But there were causes – in the town they gave
Fire, food, and comfort, to the gentle slave;
And though stern Peter, with a cruel hand,
And knotted rope, enforced the rude command,
Yet he consider'd what he'd lately felt,
And his vile blows with selfish pity dealt.
      One day such draughts the cruel fisher made,
He could not vend them in his borough-trade,
But sail'd for London-mart: the boy was ill,   140
But ever humbled to his master's will;

And on the river, where they smoothly sail'd,
He strove with terror and awhile prevail'd;
But new to danger on the angry sea,
He clung affright'd to his master's knee:
The boat grew leaky and the wind was strong,
Rough was the passage and the time was long;
His liquor fail'd, and Peter's wrath arose, –
No more is known – the rest we must suppose,
Or learn of Peter; – Peter says, he "spied   150
"The stripling's danger and for harbour tried;
"Meantime the fish, and then th'apprentice died."
    The pitying women raised a clamour round,
And weeping said, "Thou hast thy 'prentice drown'd."
    Now the stern man was summon'd to the hall,
To tell his tale before the burghers all:
He gave th'account; profess'd the lad he loved,
And kept his brazen features all unmoved.
    The mayor himself with tone severe replied, –
"Henceforth with thee shall never boy abide;   160
"Hire thee a freeman, whom thou durst not beat,
"But who, in thy despite, will sleep and eat:
"Free thou art now! – again shouldst thou appear,
"Thou'lt find thy sentence, like thy soul, severe."
    Alas! for Peter not a helping hand,
So was he hated, could he now command;
Alone he row'd his boat, alone he cast
His nets beside, or made his anchor fast;
To hold a rope or hear a curse was none, –
He toil'd and rail'd; he groan'd and swore alone.   170
    Thus by himself compell'd to live each day,
To wait for certain hours the tide's delay;
At the same times the same dull views to see,
The bounding marsh-bank and the blighted tree;
The water only, when the tides were high,
When low, the mud half-cover'd and half-dry;
The sun-burnt tar that blisters on the planks,

81

And bank-side stakes in their uneven ranks;
Heaps of entangled weeds that slowly float,
As the tide rolls by the impeded boat.   180
    When tides were neap, and, in the sultry day,
Through the tall bounding mud-banks made their way,
Which on each side rose swelling, and below
The dark warm flood ran silently and slow;
There anchoring, Peter chose from man to hide,
There hang his head, and view the lazy tide
In its hot slimy channel slowly glide;
Where the small eels that left the deeper way
For the warm shore, within the shallows play;
Where gaping muscles, left upon the mud,   190
Slope their slow passage to the fallen flood; –
Here dull and hopeless he'd lie down and trace
How sidelong crabs had scrawl'd their crooked race;
Or sadly listen to the tuneless cry
Of fishing gull or clanging golden-eye;
What time the sea-birds to the marsh would come,
And the loud bittern, from the bull-rush home,
Gave from the salt-ditch side the bellowing boom:
He nursed the feelings these dull scenes produce,
And loved to stop beside the opening sluice;   200
Where the small stream, confined in narrow bound,
Ran with a dull, unvaried, sadd'ning sound;
Where all, presented to the eye or ear,
Oppress'd the soul with misery, grief, and fear.
    Besides these objects, there were places three,
Which Peter seem'd with certain dread to see;
When he drew near them he would turn from each,
And loudly whistle till he pass'd the reach.
    A change of scene to him brought no relief;
In town, 'twas plain, men took him for a thief: 210
The sailors' wives would stop him in the street,
And say, "Now, Peter, thou'st no boy to beat:"
Infants at play, when they perceived him, ran,

Warning each other – "That's the wicked man:"
He growl'd an oath, and in an angry tone
Cursed the whole place and wish'd to be alone.

Alone he was, the same dull scenes in view,
And still more gloomy in his sight they grew:
Though man he hated, yet employ'd alone
At bootless labour, he would swear and groan,   220
Cursing the shoals that glided by the spot,
And gulls that caught them when his arts could not.

Cold nervous tremblings shook his sturdy frame,
And strange disease – he couldn't say the name;
Wild were his dreams, and oft he rose in fright,
Waked by his view of horrors in the night, –
Horrors that would the sternest minds amaze,
Horrors that demons might be proud to raise:
And though he felt forsaken, grieved at heart,
To think he lived from all mankind apart;   230
Yet, if a man approach'd, in terrors he would start.

A winter pass'd since Peter saw the town,
And summer-lodgers were again come down;
These, idly curious, with their glasses spied
The ships in bay as anchor'd for the tide, –
The river's craft, – the bustle of the quay, –
And sea-port views, which landmen love to see.

One, up the river, had a man and boat
Seen day by day, now anchor'd, now afloat;
Fisher he seem'd, yet used no net nor hook;   240
Of sea-fowl swimming by no heed he took,
But on the gliding waves still fix'd his lazy look:
At certain stations he would view the stream,
As if he stood bewilder'd in a dream,
Or that some power had chain'd him for a time,
To feel a curse or meditate on crime.

This known, some curious, some in pity went,
And others question'd – "Wretch, dost thou repent?"
He heard, he trembled, and in fear resign'd

83

His boat: new terror fill'd his restless mind; 250
Furious he grew, and up the country ran,
And there they seized him – a distemper'd man: –
Him we received, and to a parish-bed,
Follow'd and cursed, the groaning man was led.

Here when they saw him, whom they used to shun,
A lost, lone man, so harass'd and undone;
Our gentle females, ever prompt to feel,
Perceived compassion on their anger steal;
His crimes they could not from their memories blot,
But they were grieved, and trembled at his lot. 260
A priest too came, to whom his words are told;
And all the signs they shudder'd to behold.

"Look! look!" they cried; "his limbs with horror shake,
"And as he grinds his teeth, what noise they make!
"How glare his angry eyes, and yet he's not awake:
"See! what cold drops upon his forehead stand,
"And how he clenches that broad bony hand."

The priest attending, found he spoke at times
As one alluding to his fears and crimes:
"It was the fall," he mutter'd, "I can show 270
"The manner how – I never struck a blow:" –
And then aloud – "Unhand me, free my chain;
"On oath, he fell – it struck him to the brain: –
"Why ask my father? – that old man will swear
"Against my life; besides he wasn't there: –
"What, all agreed? – Am I to die to-day? –
"My Lord, in mercy, give me time to pray."

Then, as they watch'd him, calmer he became,
And grew so weak he couldn't move his frame,
But murmuring spake, – while they could see and hear 280
The start of terror and the groan of fear;
See the large dew-beads on his forehead rise,
And the cold death-drop glaze his sunken eyes;
Nor yet he died, but with unwonted force
Seem'd with some fancied being to discourse:

He knew not us, or with accustom'd art
He hid the knowledge, yet exposed his heart;
'Twas part confession and the rest defence,
A madman's tale, with gleams of waking sense.

    "I'll tell you all," he said, "the very day   290
"When the old man first placed them in my way:
"My father's spirit – he who always tried
"To give me trouble, when he lived and died –
"When he was gone, he could not be content
"To see my days in painful labour spent,
"But would appoint his meetings, and he made
"Me watch at these, and so neglect my trade.

    "'Twas one hot noon, all silent, still, serene,
"No living being had I lately seen;
"I paddled up and down and dipp'd my net,   300
"But (such his pleasure) I could nothing get, –
"A father's pleasure, when his toil was done,
"To plague and torture thus an only son!
"And so I sat and look'd upon the stream,
"How it ran on, and felt as in a dream:
"But dream it was not; no! – I fix'd my eyes
"On the mid stream and saw the spirits rise;
"I saw my father on the water stand,
"And hold a thin pale boy in either hand;
"And there they glided ghastly on the top   310
"Of the salt flood, and never touch'd a drop:
"I would have struck them, but they knew th'intent,
"And smiled upon the oar, and down they went.

    "Now, from that day, whenever I began
"To dip my net, there stood the hard old man –
"He and those boys: I humbled me and pray'd
"They would be gone; – they heeded not, but stay'd:
"Nor could I turn, nor would the boat go by,
"But gazing on the spirits, there was I:
"They bade me leap to death, but I was loth to die: 320
"And every day, as sure as day arose,

85

"Would these three spirits meet me ere the close;
"To hear and mark them daily was my doom,
"And 'Come,' they said, with weak, sad voices, 'come.'
"To row away with all my strength I try'd,
"But there were they, hard by me in the tide,
"The three unbodied forms – and 'Come,' still 'come,' they cried
    "Fathers should pity – but this old man shook
"His hoary locks, and froze me by a look:
"Thrice, when I struck them, through the water came   330
"A hollow groan, that weaken'd all my frame:
"'Father!' said I, 'have mercy:' – He replied,
"I know not what – the angry spirit lied, –
"'Didst thou not draw thy knife?' said he: – 'Twas true,
"But I had pity and my arm withdrew:
"He cried for mercy which I kindly gave,
"But he has no compassion in his grave.
    "There were three places, where they ever rose, –
"The whole long river has not such as those, –
"Places accursed, where, if a man remain,   340
"He'll see the things which strike him to the brain;
"And there they made me on my paddle lean,
"And look at them for hours; – accursed scene!
"When they would glide to that smooth eddy-space,
"Then bid me leap and join them in the place;
"And at my groans each little villain sprite
"Enjoy'd my pains and vanish'd in delight.
    "In one fierce summer-day, when my poor brain
"Was burning hot and cruel was my pain,
"Then came this father-foe, and there he stood   350
"With his two boys again upon the flood;
"There was more mischief in their eyes, more glee
"In their pale faces when they glared at me:
"Still did they force me on the oar to rest,
"And when they saw me fainting and oppress'd,
"He, with his hand, the old man, scoop'd the flood,
"And there came flame about him mix'd with blood;

"He bade me stoop and look upon the place,
"Then flung the hot-red liquor in my face;
"Burning it blazed, and then I roar'd for pain,   360
"I thought the demons would have turn'd my brain.
  "Still there they stood, and forced me to behold
"A place of horrors – they cannot be told –
"Where the flood open'd, there I heard the shriek
"Of tortured guilt – no earthly tongue can speak:
"'All days alike! for ever!' did they say,
"'And unremitted torments every day' –
"Yes, so they said:" – But here he ceased and gazed
On all around, affrighten'd and amazed;
And still he tried to speak, and look'd in dread   370
Of frighten'd females gathering round his bed;
Then dropp'd exhausted and appear'd at rest,
Till the strong foe the vital powers possess'd;
Then with an inward, broken voice he cried,
"Again they come," and mutter'd as he died.

Tales

The Dumb Orators

That all men would be cowards if they dare,
Some men we know have courage to declare;
And this the life of many an hero shows,
That like the tide, man's courage ebbs and flows:
With friends and gay companions round them, then
Men boldly speak and have the hearts of men;
Who, with opponents seated, miss the aid
Of kind applauding looks, and grow afraid;
Like timid trav'llers in the night, they fear
Th'assault of foes, when not a friend is near.   10

    In contest mighty and of conquest proud
Was Justice Bolt, impetuous, warm, and loud;
His fame, his prowess all the country knew,
And disputants, with one so fierce, were few:
He was a younger son, for law design'd,
With dauntless look and persevering mind;
While yet a clerk, for disputation famed,
No efforts tired him, and no conflicts tamed.

    Scarcely he bade his master's desk adieu,
When both his brothers from the world withdrew.   20
An ample fortune he from them possess'd,
And was with saving care and prudence bless'd.
Now would he go and to the country give
Example how an English 'squire should live;
How bounteous, yet how frugal man may be,
By a well-order'd hospitality;
He would the rights of all so well maintain,
That none should idle be, and none complain.

    All this and more he purposed – and what man
Could do, he did to realize his plan: 30
But time convinced him that we cannot keep

A breed of reasoners like a flock of sheep;
For they, so far from following as we lead,
Make that a cause why they will not proceed.
Man will not follow where a rule is shown,
But loves to take a method of his own;
Explain the way with all your care and skill,
This will he quit, if but to prove he will. –
Yet had our Justice honour – and the crowd,
Awed by his presence, their respect avow'd.   40

    In later years he found his heart incline,
More than in youth, to gen'rous food and wine;
But no indulgence check'd the powerful love
He felt to teach, to argue, and reprove.

    Meetings, or public calls, he never miss'd –
To dictate often, always to assist.
Oft he the clergy join'd, and not a cause
Pertain'd to them but he could quote the laws;
He upon tithes and residence display'd
A fund of knowledge for the hearer's aid;   50
And could on glebe and farming, wool and grain,
A long discourse, without a pause, maintain.

    To his experience and his native sense
He join'd a bold imperious eloquence;
The grave, stern look of men inform'd and wise,
A full command of feature, heart, and eyes,
An awe-compelling frown, and fear-inspiring size.
When at the table, not a guest was seen
With appetite so ling'ring, or so keen;
But when the outer man no more required,   60
The inner waked, and he was man inspired.
His subjects then were those, a subject true
Presents in fairest form to public view;
Of Church and State, of Law, with mighty strength
Of words he spoke, in speech of mighty length:
And now, into the vale of years declined,
He hides too little of the monarch-mind:

He kindles anger by untimely jokes,
And opposition by contempt provokes;
Mirth he suppresses by his awful frown,   70
And humble spirits, by disdain, keeps down;
Blamed by the mild, approved by the severe,
The prudent fly him, and the valiant fear.
   For overbearing is his proud discourse,
And overwhelming of his voice the force;
And overpowering is he when he shows
What floats upon a mind that always overflows.
   This ready man at every meeting rose,
Something to hint, determine, or propose;
And grew so fond of teaching, that he taught   80
Those who instruction needed not or sought:
Happy our hero, when he could excite
Some thoughtless talker to the wordy fight:
Let him a subject at his pleasure choose,
Physic or Law, Religion or the Muse;
On all such themes he was prepared to shine,
Physician, poet, lawyer, and divine.
Hemm'd in by some tough argument, borne down
By press of language and the awful frown,
In vain for mercy shall the culprit plead;   90
His crime is past, and sentence must proceed:
Ah! suffering man, have patience, bear thy woes –
For lo! the clock – at ten the Justice goes.
   This powerful man, on business or to please
A curious taste, or weary grown of ease,
On a long journey travell'd many a mile
Westward, and halted midway in our isle;
Content to view a city large and fair,
Though none had notice – what a man was there!
   Silent two days, he then began to long   100
Again to try a voice so loud and strong;
To give his favourite topics some new grace,
And gain some glory in such distant place;

To reap some present pleasure, and to sow
Seeds of fair fame, in after-time to grow:
Here will men say, "We heard, at such an hour,
"The best of speakers – wonderful his power."
    Inquiry made, he found that day would meet
A learned club, and in the very street:
Knowledge to gain and give, was the design;   110
To speak, to hearken, to debate, and dine:
This pleased our traveller, for he felt his force
In either way, to eat or to discourse.
    Nothing more easy than to gain access
To men like these, with his polite address:
So he succeeded, and first look'd around,
To view his objects and to take his ground;
And therefore silent chose awhile to sit,
Then enter boldly by some lucky hit;
Some observation keen or stroke severe,   120
To cause some wonder or excite some fear.
    Now, dinner past, no longer he suppress'd
His strong dislike to be a silent guest;
Subjects and words were now at his command –
When disappointment frown'd on all he plann'd;
For, hark! – he heard amazed, on every side,
His church insulted and her priests belied;
The laws reviled, the ruling power abused,
The land derided, and its foes excused: –
He heard and ponder'd. – What, to men so vile,   130
Should be his language? For his threat'ning style
They were too many; – if his speech were meek,
They would despise such poor attempts to speak:
At other times with every word at will,
He now sat lost, perplex'd, astonish'd, still.
    Here were Socinians, Deists, and indeed
All who, as foes to England's church, agreed;
But still with creeds unlike, and some without a creed:
Here, too, fierce friends of liberty he saw,

Who own'd no prince and who obey no law;   140
There were Reformers of each different sort,
Foes to the laws, the priesthood, and the court;
Some on their favourite plans alone intent,
Some purely angry and malevolent:
The rash were proud to blame their country's laws;
The vain, to seem supporters of a cause;
One call'd for change that he would dread to see;
Another sigh'd for Gallic liberty!
And numbers joining with the forward crew,
For no one reason – but that numbers do.   150
    "How," said the Justice, "can this trouble rise,
"This shame and pain, from creatures I despise?"
And conscience answer'd – "The prevailing cause
"Is thy delight in listening to applause;
"Here, thou art seated with a tribe, who spurn
"Thy favourite themes, and into laughter turn
"Thy fears and wishes; silent and obscure,
"Thyself, shalt thou the long harangue endure;
"And learn, by feeling, what it is to force
"On thy unwilling friends the long discourse: 160
"What though thy thoughts be just, and these, it seems,
"Are traitors' projects, idiots' empty schemes;
"Yet minds like bodies cramm'd, reject their food,
"Nor will be forced and tortured for their good!"
    At length, a sharp, shrewd, sallow man arose,
And begg'd he briefly might his mind disclose;
"It was his duty, in these worst of times,
"T'inform the govern'd of their rulers' crimes:"
This pleasant subject to attend, they each
Prepared to listen, and forebore to teach.   170
    Then voluble and fierce the wordy man
Through a long chain of favourite horrors ran: –
First, of the church, from whose enslaving power
He was deliver'd, and he bless'd the hour;
"Bishops and deans, and prebendaries all,"

He said, "were cattle fatt'ning in the stall;
"Slothful and pursy, insolent and mean,
"Were every bishop, prebendary, dean,
"And wealthy rector: curates, poorly paid,
"Were only dull; – he would not them upbraid."   180
  From priests he turn'd to canons, creeds, and prayers,
Rubrics and rules, and all our church affairs;
Churches themselves, desk, pulpit, altar, all
The Justice reverenced – and pronounced their fall.
  Then from religion Hammond turn'd his view,
To give our rulers the correction due;
Not one wise action had these triflers plann'd;
There was, it seem'd, no wisdom in the land;
Save in this patriot tribe, who meet at times
To show the statesman's errors and his crimes.   190
  Now here was Justice Bolt compell'd to sit,
To hear the deist's scorn, the rebel's wit;   (
The fact mis-stated, the envenom'd lie,
And staring, spell-bound, made not one reply.
  Then were our laws abused – and with the laws,
All who prepare, defend, or judge a cause:
"We have no lawyer whom a man can trust,"
Proceeded Hammond – "if the laws were just;
  "But they are evil; 'tis the savage state
"Is only good, and ours sophisticate!   200
"See! the free creatures in their woods and plains,
"Where without laws each happy monarch reigns,
"King of himself – while we a number dread,
"By slaves commanded and by dunces led;
"Oh, let the name with either state agree –
"Savage our own we'll name, and civil theirs shall be."
  The silent Justice still astonish'd sate,
And wonder'd much whom he was gazing at;
Twice he essay'd to speak – but in a cough
The faint, indignant, dying speech went off: 210
"But who is this?" thought he – "a dæmon vile,

93

"With wicked meaning and a vulgar style:
"Hammond they call him; they can give the name
"Of man to devils. – Why am I so tame?
"Why crush I not the viper?" – Fear replied,
"Watch him awhile, and let his strength be tried;
"He will be foil'd, if man; but if his aid
"Be from beneath, 'tis well to be afraid."
    "We are call'd free!" said Hammond – "doleful times
"When rulers add their insult to their crimes;   220
"For should our scorn expose each powerful vice,
"It would be libel, and we pay the price."
    Thus with licentious words the man went on,
Proving that liberty of speech was gone;
That all were slaves – nor had we better chance
For better times than as allies to France.
    Loud groan'd the stranger – Why, he must relate;
And own'd, "In sorrow for his country's fate;"
"Nay, she were safe," the ready man replied,
"Might patriots rule her, and could reasoners guide;   230
"When all to vote, to speak, to teach, are free,
"Whate'er their creeds or their opinions be;
"When books of statutes are consumed in flames,
"And courts and copyholds are empty names;
"Then will be times of joy – but ere they come,
"Havock, and war, and blood must be our doom."
    The man here paused – then loudly for reform
He call'd, and hail'd the prospect of the storm;
The wholesome blast, the fertilizing flood –
Peace gain'd by tumult, plenty bought with blood: 240
Sharp means, he own'd; but when the land's disease
Asks cure complete, no med'cines are like these.
    Our Justice now, more led by fear than rage,
Saw it in vain with madness to engage;
With imps of darkness no man seeks to fight,
Knaves to instruct, or set deceivers right:
Then as the daring speech denounced these woes,

Sick at the soul, the grieving guest arose;
Quick on the board his ready cash he threw,
And from the dæmons to his closet flew: 250
There when secured, he pray'd with earnest zeal,
That all they wish'd these patriot-souls might feel;
"Let them to France, their darling country, haste,
"And all the comforts of a Frenchman taste;
"Let them his safety, freedom, pleasure know,
"Feel all their rulers on the land bestow;
"And be at length dismiss'd by one unerring blow;
"Not hack'd and hew'd by one afraid to strike,
"But shorn by that which shears all men alike;
"Nor, as in Britain, let them curse delay   260
"Of law, but borne without a form away –
"Suspected, tried, condemn'd, and carted in a day;
"Oh! let them taste what they so much approve,
"These strong fierce freedoms of the land they love."
   Home came our hero, to forget no more
The fear he felt and ever must deplore:
For though he quickly join'd his friends again,
And could with decent force his themes maintain,
Still it occurr'd that, in a luckless time,
He fail'd to fight with heresy and crime;   270
It was observed his words were not so strong,
His tones so powerful, his harangues so long,
As in old times – for he would often drop
The lofty look, and of a sudden stop;
When conscience whisper'd, that he once was still,
And let the wicked triumph at their will;
And therefore now, when not a foe was near,
He had no right so valiant to appear.
   Some years had pass'd, and he perceived his fears
Yield to the spirit of his earlier years –   280
When at a meeting, with his friends beside,
He saw an object that awaked his pride;
His shame, wrath, vengeance, indignation – all

Man's harsher feelings did that sight recall.
    For lo! beneath him fix'd, our man of law
That lawless man the foe of order saw;
Once fear'd, now scorn'd; once dreaded, now abhorr'd;
A wordy man, and evil every word:
Again he gazed – "It is," said he, "the same;
"Caught and secure: his master owes him shame:"   290
So thought our hero, who each instant found
His courage rising, from the numbers round.
    As when a felon has escaped and fled,
So long, that law conceives the culprit dead;
And back recall'd her myrmidons, intent
On some new game, and with a stronger scent;
Till she beholds him in a place, where none
Could have conceived the culprit would have gone;
There he sits upright in his seat, secure,
As one whose conscience is correct and pure;   300
This rouses anger for the old offence,
And scorn for all such seeming and pretence;
So on this Hammond look'd our hero bold,
Rememb'ring well that vile offence of old;
And now he saw the rebel dared t'intrude
Among the pure, the loyal, and the good;
The crime provoked his wrath, the folly stirr'd his blood:
Nor wonder was it if so strange a sight
Caused joy with vengeance, terror with delight;
Terror like this a tiger might create,   310
A joy like this to see his captive state,
At once to know his force and then decree his fate.
    Hammond, much praised by numerous friends, was come
To read his lectures, so admired at home;
Historic lectures, where he loved to mix
His free plain hints on modern politics:
Here, he had heard, that numbers had design,
Their business finish'd, to sit down and dine;
This gave him pleasure, for he judged it right

To show by day, that he could speak at night.   320
Rash the design – for he perceived, too late,
Not one approving friend beside him sate;
The greater number, whom he traced around,
Were men in black, and he conceived they frown'd.
"I will not speak," he thought; "no pearls of mine
"Shall be presented to this herd of swine;"
Not this avail'd him, when he cast his eye
On Justice Bolt; he could not fight, nor fly:
He saw a man to whom he gave the pain,
Which now he felt must be return'd again;   330
His conscience told him with what keen delight
He, at that time, enjoy'd a stranger's fright;
That stranger now befriended – he alone,
For all his insult, friendless, to atone;
Now he could feel it cruel that a heart
Should be distress'd, and none to take its part;
"Though one by one," said Pride, "I would defy
"Much greater men, yet meeting every eye,
"I do confess a fear – but he will pass me by."
    Vain hope! the Justice saw the foe's distress,   340
With exultation he could not suppress;
He felt the fish was hook'd – and so forebore,
In playful spite, to draw it to the shore.
Hammond look'd round again; but none were near,
With friendly smile, to still his growing fear;
But all above him seem'd a solemn row
Of priests and deacons, so they seem'd below;
He wonder'd who his right-hand man might be –
Vicar of Holt cum Uppingham was he;
And who the man of that dark frown possess'd –   350
Rector of Bradley and of Barton-west;
"A pluralist," he growl'd – but check'd the word,
That warfare might not, by his zeal, be stirr'd.
    But now began the man above to show
Fierce looks and threat'nings to the man below;

97

Who had some thoughts his peace by flight to seek –
But how then lecture, if he dared not speak! –
    Now as the Justice for the war prepared,
He seem'd just then to question if he dared;
"He may resist, although his power be small,   360
"And growing desperate may defy us all;
"One dog attack, and he prepares for flight –
"Resist another, and he strives to bite;
"Nor can I say, if this rebellious cur
"Will fly for safety, or will scorn to stir."
Alarm'd by this, he lash'd his soul to rage,
Burn'd with strong shame, and hurried to engage.
    As a male turkey straggling on the green,
When by fierce harriers, terriers, mongrels seen,
He feels the insult of the noisy train,   370
And sculks aside, though moved by much disdain;
But when that turkey, at his own barn-door,
Sees one poor straying puppy and no more,
(A foolish puppy who had left the pack,
Thoughtless what foe was threat'ning at his back,)
He moves about, as ship prepared to sail,
He hoists his proud rotundity of tail,
The half-seal'd eyes and changeful neck he shows,
Where, in its quick'ning colours, vengeance glows;
From red to blue the pendant wattles turn,   380
Blue mix'd with red, as matches when they burn;
And thus th'intruding snarler to oppose,
Urged by enkindling wrath, he gobbling goes.
    So look'd our hero in his wrath, his cheeks
Flush'd with fresh fires and glow'd in tingling streaks;
His breath by passion's force awhile restrain'd,
Like a stopp'd current, greater force regain'd;
So spoke, so look'd he, every eye and ear
Were fix'd to view him, or were turn'd to hear.
    "My friends, you know me, you can witness all,   390
"How urged by passion, I restrain my gall;

"And every motive to revenge withstand –
"Save when I hear abused my native land.

   "Is it not known, agreed, confirm'd, confess'd,
"That of all people, we are govern'd best?
"We have the force of monarchies; are free,
"As the most proud republicans can be;
"And have those prudent counsels that arise
"In grave and cautious aristocracies;
"And live there those, in such all-glorious state,   400
"Traitors protected in the land they hate?
"Rebels, still warring with the laws that give
"To them subsistence? – Yes, such wretches live.

   "Ours is a church reform'd, and now no more
"Is aught for man to mend or to restore;
"'Tis pure in doctrines, 'tis correct in creeds,
"Has nought redundant, and it nothing needs;
"No evil is therein – no wrinkle, spot,
"Stain, blame, or blemish: – I affirm there's not.

   "All this you know – now mark what once befell,   410
"With grief I bore it, and with shame I tell;
"I was entrapp'd – yes, so it came to pass,
"'Mid heathen rebels, a tumultuous class;
"Each to his country bore a hellish mind,
"Each like his neighbour was of cursed kind;
"The land that nursed them they blasphemed; the laws,
"Their sovereign's glory, and their country's cause;
"And who their mouth, their master-fiend, and who
"Rebellion's oracle? – You, caitiff, you!"
   He spoke, and standing stretch'd his mighty arm,   420
And fix'd the man of words, as by a charm.

   "How raved that railer! Sure some hellish power
"Restrained my tongue in that delirious hour,
"Or I had hurl'd the shame and vengeance due
"On him, the guide of that infuriate crew;
"But to mine eyes such dreadful looks appear'd,
"Such mingled yell of lying words I heard,

"That I conceived around were dæmons all,
"And till I fled the house, I fear'd its fall.
    "Oh! could our country from our coasts expel   430
"Such foes! to nourish those who wish her well:
"This her mild laws forbid, but we may still
"From us eject them by our sovereign will;
"This let us do." – He said, and then began
A gentler feeling for the silent man;
Ev'n in our hero's mighty soul arose
A touch of pity for experienced woes;
But this was transient, and with angry eye
He sternly look'd, and paused for a reply.
    'Twas then the man of many words would speak –   440
But, in his trial, had them all to seek:
To find a friend he look'd the circle round,
But joy or scorn in every feature found;
He sipp'd his wine, but in those times of dread
Wine only adds confusion to the head;
In doubt he reason'd with himself – "And how
"Harangue at night, if I be silent now?"
From pride and praise received, he sought to draw
Courage to speak, but still remain'd the awe;
One moment rose he with a forced disdain,   450
And then abash'd, sunk sadly down again;
While in our hero's glance he seem'd to read,
"Slave and insurgent! what hast thou to plead?" –
    By desperation urged, he now began:
"I seek no favour – I – the Rights of Man!
"Claim; and I – nay! – but give me leave – and I
"Insist – a man – that is – and in reply,
"I speak." – Alas! each new attempt was vain:
Confused he stood, he sate, he rose again;
At length he growl'd defiance, sought the door,   460
Cursed the whole synod, and was seen no more.
    "Laud we," said Justice Bolt," the Powers above;
"Thus could our speech the sturdiest foe remove."

Exulting now he gain'd new strength of fame,
And lost all feelings of defeat and shame.
    "He dared not strive, you witness'd – dared not lift
"His voice, nor drive at his accursed drift:
"So all shall tremble, wretches who oppose
"Our church or state – thus be it to our foes."
    He spoke, and, seated with his former air,   470
Look'd his full self, and fill'd his ample chair;
Took one full bumper to each favourite cause,
And dwelt all night on politics and laws,
With high applauding voice, that gain'd him high applause.

The Parting Hour

Minutely trace man's life; year after year,
Through all his days let all his deeds appear,
And then, though some may in that life be strange,
Yet there appears no vast nor sudden change:
The links that bind those various deeds are seen,
And no mysterious void is left between.
    But let these binding links be all destroy'd,
All that through years he suffer'd or enjoy'd;
Let that vast gap be made, and then behold –
This was the youth, and he is thus when old;   10
Then we at once the work of Time survey,
And in an instant see a life's decay;
Pain mix'd with pity in our bosoms rise,
And sorrow takes new sadness from surprise.
    Beneath yon tree, observe an ancient pair –
A sleeping man; a woman in her chair,
Watching his looks with kind and pensive air;
No wife, nor sister she, nor is the name
Nor kindred of this friendly pair the same;
Yet so allied are they, that few can feel   20

101

Her constant, warm, unwearied, anxious zeal;
Their years and woes, although they long have loved,
Keep their good name and conduct unreproved;
Thus life's small comforts they together share,
And while life lingers for the grave prepare.
　　No other subjects on their spirits press,
Nor gain such int'rest as the past distress;
Grievous events that from the mem'ry drive
Life's common cares, and those alone survive,
Mix with each thought, in every action share,　　30
Darken each dream, and blend with every prayer.
　　To David Booth, his fourth and last-born boy,
Allen his name, was more than common joy;
And as the child grew up, there seem'd in him
A more than common life in every limb;
A strong and handsome stripling he became,
And the gay spirit answer'd to the frame;
A lighter, happier lad was never seen,
For ever easy, cheerful, or serene;
His early love he fix'd upon a fair　　40
And gentle maid – they were a handsome pair.
　　They at an infant-school together play'd,
Where the foundation of their love was laid;
The boyish champion would his choice attend
In every sport, in every fray defend.
As prospects open'd and as life advanced,
They walk'd together, they together danced;
On all occasions, from their early years,
They mix'd their joys and sorrows, hopes and fears;
Each heart was anxious, till it could impart　　50
Its daily feelings to its kindred heart;
As years increased, unnumber'd petty wars
Broke out between them; jealousies and jars;
Causeless indeed, and follow'd by a peace,
That gave to love – growth, vigour, and increase.
Whilst yet a boy, when other minds are void,

Domestic thoughts young Allen's hours employ'd;
Judith in gaining hearts had no concern,
Rather intent the matron's part to learn;
Thus early prudent and sedate they grew,   60
While lovers, thoughtful – and though children, true.
To either parents not a day appear'd,
When with this love they might have interfered:
Childish at first, they cared not to restrain;
And strong at last, they saw restriction vain;
Nor knew they when that passion to reprove –
Now idle fondness, now resistless love.
    So while the waters rise, the children tread
On the broad estuary's sandy bed;
But soon the channel fills, from side to side   70
Comes danger rolling with the deep'ning tide;
Yet none who saw the rapid current flow
Could the first instant of that danger know.
    The lovers waited till the time should come
When they together could possess a home:
In either house were men and maids unwed,
Hopes to be soothed, and tempers to be led.
Then Allen's mother of his favourite maid
Spoke from the feelings of a mind afraid:
"Dress and amusements were her sole employ,"   80
She said – "entangling her deluded boy;"
And yet, in truth, a mother's jealous love
Had much imagined and could little prove;
Judith had beauty – and if vain, was kind,
Discreet, and mild, and had a serious mind.
    Dull was their prospect – when the lovers met,
They said, we must not – dare not venture yet:
"Oh! could I labour for thee," Allen cried,
"Why should our friends be thus dissatisfied?
"On my own arm I could depend, but they   90
"Still urge obedience – must I yet obey?"
Poor Judith felt the grief, but grieving begg'd delay.

103

At length a prospect came that seem'd to smile,
And faintly woo them, from a Western Isle;
A kinsman there a widow's hand had gain'd,
"Was old, was rich, and childless yet remain'd;
"Would some young Booth to his affairs attend,
"And wait awhile, he might expect a friend."
The elder brothers, who were not in love,
Fear'd the false seas, unwilling to remove;   100
But the young Allen, an enamour'd boy,
Eager an independence to enjoy,
Would through all perils seek it, – by the sea, –
Through labour, danger, pain, or slavery.
The faithful Judith his design approved,
For both were sanguine, they were young and loved.
The mother's slow consent was then obtain'd;
The time arrived, to part alone remain'd:
All things prepared, on the expected day
Was seen the vessel anchor'd in the bay,   110
From her would seamen in the evening come,
To take th'adventurous Allen from his home;
With his own friends the final day he pass'd,
And every painful hour, except the last.
The grieving father urged the cheerful glass,
To make the moments with less sorrow pass;
Intent the mother look'd upon her son,
And wish'd th'assent withdrawn, the deed undone;
The younger sister, as he took his way,
Hung on his coat, and begg'd for more delay: 120
But his own Judith call'd him to the shore,
Whom he must meet, for they might meet no more; –
And there he found her – faithful, mournful, true,
Weeping and waiting for a last adieu!
The ebbing tide had left the sand, and there
Moved with slow steps the melancholy pair:
Sweet were the painful moments – but how sweet,
And without pain, when they again should meet!

Now either spoke, as hope and fear impress'd
Each their alternate triumph in the breast.   130
    Distance alarm'd the maid – she cried, "'Tis far!"
And danger too – "it is a time of war:
"Then in those countries are diseases strange,
"And women gay, and men are prone to change;
"What then may happen in a year, when things
"Of vast importance every moment brings!
"But hark! an oar!" she cried, yet none appear'd –
'Twas love's mistake, who fancied what it fear'd;
And she continued – "Do, my Allen, keep
"Thy heart from evil, let thy passions sleep;   140
"Believe it good, nay glorious, to prevail,
"And stand in safety where so many fail;
"And do not, Allen, or for shame, or pride,
"Thy faith abjure, or thy profession hide;
"Can I believe *his* love will lasting prove,
"Who has no rev'rence for the God I love?
"I know thee well! how good thou art and kind;
"But strong the passions that invade thy mind. –
"Now, what to me hath Allen to commend?" –
"Upon my mother," said the youth, "attend;   150
"Forget her spleen, and in my place appear;
"Her love to me will make my Judith dear:
"Oft I shall think, (such comfort lovers seek),
"Who speaks of me, and fancy what they speak;
"Then write on all occasions, always dwell
"On hope's fair prospects, and be kind and well,
"And ever choose the fondest, tenderest style."
She answer'd, "No," but answer'd with a smile.
"And now, my Judith, at so sad a time,
"Forgive my fear, and call it not my crime;   160
"When with our youthful neighbours 'tis thy chance
"To meet in walks, the visit or the dance,
"When every lad would on my lass attend,
"Choose not a smooth designer for a friend;

"That fawning Philip! – nay, be not severe,
"A rival's hope must cause a lover's fear."
    Displeased she felt, and might in her reply
Have mix'd some anger, but the boat was nigh,
Now truly heard! – it soon was full in sight; –
Now the sad farewell, and the long good-night;   170
For, see! – his friends come hast'ning to the beach,
And now the gunwale is within the reach;
"Adieu! – farewell! – remember!" – and what more
Affection taught, was utter'd from the shore!
But Judith left them with a heavy heart,
Took a last view, and went to weep apart!
And now his friends went slowly from the place,
Where she stood still, the dashing oar to trace,
Till all were silent! – for the youth she pray'd,
And softly then return'd the weeping maid.   180
    They parted, thus by hope and fortune led,
And Judith's hours in pensive pleasure fled;
But when return'd the youth? – the youth no more
Return'd exulting to his native shore;
But forty years were past, and then there came
A worn-out man with wither'd limbs and lame,
His mind oppress'd with woes, and bent with age his frame:
Yes! old and grieved, and trembling with decay,
Was Allen landing in his native bay,
Willing his breathless form should blend with kindred clay.   190
In an autumnal eve he left the beach,
In such an eve he chanced the port to reach:
He was alone; he press'd the very place
Of the sad parting, of the last embrace:
There stood his parents, there retired the maid,
So fond, so tender, and so much afraid;
And on that spot, through many a year, his mind
Turn'd mournful back, half sinking, half resign'd.
    No one was present; of its crew bereft,
A single boat was in the billows left;   200

106

Sent from some anchor'd vessel in the bay,
At the returning tide to sail away:
O'er the black stern the moonlight softly play'd,
The loosen'd foresail flapping in the shade;
All silent else on shore; but from the town
A drowsy peal of distant bells came down:
From the tall houses here and there, a light
Served some confused remembrance to excite:
"There," he observed, and new emotions felt,
"Was my first home – and yonder Judith dwelt;   210
"Dead! dead are all! I long – I fear to know,"
He said, and walk'd impatient, and yet slow.
    Sudden there broke upon his grief a noise
Of merry tumult and of vulgar joys:
Seamen returning to their ship, were come,
With idle numbers straying from their home;
Allen among them mix'd, and in the old
Strove some familiar features to behold;
While fancy aided memory: – "Man! what cheer?"
A sailor cried; "Art thou at anchor here?"   220
Faintly he answer'd, and then tried to trace
Some youthful features in some aged face:
A swarthy matron he beheld, and thought
She might unfold the very truths he sought:
Confused and trembling, he the dame address'd:
"The Booths! yet live they?" pausing and oppress'd;
Then spake again: – "Is there no ancient man,
"David his name? – assist me, if you can. –
"Flemmings there were – and Judith, doth she live?"
The woman gazed, nor could an answer give;   230
Yet wond'ring stood, and all were silent by,
Feeling a strange and solemn sympathy.
The woman musing said – "She knew full well
"Where the old people came at last to dwell;
"They had a married daughter and a son,
"But they were dead, and now remain'd not one."

"Yes," said an elder, who had paused intent
On days long past, "there was a sad event; –
"One of these Booths – it was my mother's tale –
"Here left his lass, I know not where to sail: 240
"She saw their parting, and observed the pain;
"But never came th'unhappy man again:"
"The ship was captured" – Allen meekly said,
"And what became of the forsaken maid?"
The woman answer'd: "I remember now,
"She used to tell the lasses of her vow,
"And of her lover's loss, and I have seen
"The gayest hearts grow sad where she has been;
"Yet in her grief she married, and was made
"Slave to a wretch, whom meekly she obey'd   250
"And early buried – but I know no more.
"And hark! our friends are hast'ning to the shore."
     Allen soon found a lodging in the town,
And walk'd a man unnoticed up and down.
This house, and this, he knew, and thought a face
He sometimes could among a number trace:
Of names remember'd there remain'd a few,
But of no favourites, and the rest were new;
A merchant's wealth, when Allen went to sea,
Was reckon'd boundless. – Could he living be?   260
Or lived his son? for one he had, the heir
To a vast business, and a fortune fair.
No! but that heir's poor widow, from her shed,
With crutches went to take her dole of bread:
There was a friend whom he had left a boy,
With hope to sail the master of a hoy;
Him, after many a stormy day, he found
With his great wish, his life's whole purpose, crown'd.
This hoy's proud captain look'd in Allen's face, –
"Yours is, my friend," said he, "a woful case;   270
"We cannot all succeed; I now command
"The Betsy sloop, and am not much at land;

"But when we meet, you shall your story tell
"Of foreign parts – I bid you now farewell!"
    Allen so long had left his native shore,
He saw but few whom he had seen before;
The older people, as they met him, cast
A pitying look, oft speaking as they pass'd –
"The man is Allen Booth, and it appears
"He dwelt among us in his early years;   280
"We see the name engraved upon the stones,
"Where this poor wanderer means to lay his bones."
Thus where he lived and loved – unhappy change! –
He seems a stranger, and finds all are strange.
    But now a widow, in a village near,
Chanced of the melancholy man to hear;
Old as she was, to Judith's bosom came
Some strong emotions at the well-known name;
He was her much-loved Allen, she had stay'd
Ten troubled years, a sad afflicted maid;   290
Then she was wedded, of his death assured,
And much of mis'ry in her lot endured;
Her husband died; her children sought their bread
In various places, and to her were dead.
The once fond lovers met; not grief nor age,
Sickness or pain, their hearts could disengage:
Each had immediate confidence; a friend
Both now beheld, on whom they might depend:
"Now is there one to whom I can express
"My nature's weakness and my soul's distress."   300
Allen look'd up, and with impatient heart –
"Let me not lose thee – never let us part:
"So Heaven this comfort to my sufferings give,
"It is not all distress to think and live."
Thus Allen spoke – for time had not removed
The charms attach'd to one so fondly loved;
Who with more health, the mistress of their cot,
Labours to soothe the evils of his lot.

109

To her, to her alone, his various fate,
At various times, 'tis comfort to relate;   310
And yet his sorrow – she too loves to hear
What wrings her bosom, and compels the tear.
    First he related how he left the shore,
Alarm'd with fears that they should meet no more:
Then, ere the ship had reach'd her purposed course,
They met and yielded to the Spanish force;
Then 'cross th'Atlantic seas they bore their prey,
Who grieving landed from their sultry bay;
And marching many a burning league, he found
Himself a slave upon a miner's ground: 320
There a good priest his native language spoke,
And gave some ease to his tormenting yoke;
Kindly advanced him in his master's grace,
And he was station'd in an easier place:
There, hopeless ever to escape the land,
He to a Spanish maiden gave his hand;
In cottage shelter'd from the blaze of day
He saw his happy infants round him play;
Where summer shadows, made by lofty trees,
Waved o'er his seat, and soothed his reveries;   330
E'en then he thought of England, nor could sigh,
But his fond Isabel demanded, "Why?"
Grieved by the story, she the sigh repaid,
And wept in pity for the English maid:
Thus twenty years were pass'd, and pass'd his views
Of further bliss, for he had wealth to lose:
His friend now dead, some foe had dared to paint
"His faith as tainted: he his spouse would taint;
"Make all his children infidels, and found
"An English heresy on Christian ground."   340
    "Whilst I was poor," said Allen, "none would care
"What my poor notions of religion were;
"None ask'd me whom I worshipp'd, how I pray'd,
"If due obedience to the laws were paid:

"My good adviser taught me to be still,
"Nor to make converts had I power or will.
"I preach'd no foreign doctrine to my wife,
"And never mention'd Luther in my life;
"I, all they said, say what they would, allow'd,
"And when the fathers bade me bow, I bow'd,   350
"Their forms I follow'd, whether well or sick,
"And was a most obedient Catholic.
"But I had money, and these pastors found
"My notions vague, heretical, unsound:
"A wicked book they seized; the very Turk
"Could not have read a more pernicious work;
"To me pernicious, who if it were good
"Or evil question'd not, nor understood:
"Oh! had I little but the book possess'd,
"I might have read it, and enjoy'd my rest."   360
    Alas! poor Allen, through his wealth was seen
Crimes that by poverty conceal'd had been:
Faults that in dusty pictures rest unknown
Are in an instant through the varnish shown.
    He told their cruel mercy; how at last,
In Christian kindness for the merits past,
They spared his forfeit life, but bade him fly,
Or for his crime and contumacy die;
Fly from all scenes, all objects of delight:
His wife, his children, weeping in his sight,   370
All urging him to flee, he fled, and cursed his flight.
    He next related how he found a way,
Guideless and grieving, to Campeachy Bay:
There in the woods he wrought, and there, among
Some lab'ring seamen, heard his native tongue:
The sound, one moment, broke upon his pain
With joyful force; he long'd to hear again:
Again he heard; he seized an offer'd hand,
"And when beheld you last our native land?"
He cry'd, "and in what county? quickly say" –   380

111

The seamen answer'd – strangers all were they;
One only at his native port had been;
He, landing once, the quay and church had seen,
For that esteem'd; but nothing more he knew.
Still more to know, would Allen join the crew,
Sail where they sail'd, and, many a peril past,
They at his kinsman's isle their anchor cast;
But him they found not, nor could one relate
Aught of his will, his wish, or his estate.
This grieved not Allen; then again he sail'd   390
For England's coast, again his fate prevail'd:
War raged, and he, an active man and strong,
Was soon impress'd, and served his country long.
By various shores he pass'd, on various seas,
Never so happy as when void of ease. –
And then he told how in a calm distress'd,
Day after day his soul was sick of rest;
When, as a log upon the deep they stood,
Then roved his spirit to the inland wood;
Till, while awake, he dream'd, that on the seas   400
Were his loved home, the hill, the stream, the trees:
He gazed, he pointed to the scenes: – "There stand
"My wife, my children, 'tis my lovely land;
"See! there my dwelling – oh! delicious scene
"Of my best life – unhand me – are ye men?"
    And thus the frenzy ruled him, till the wind
Brush'd the fond pictures from the stagnant mind.
    He told of bloody fights, and how at length
The rage of battle gave his spirits strength:
'Twas in the Indian seas his limb he lost,   410
And he was left half-dead upon the coast;
But living gain'd, 'mid rich aspiring men,
A fair subsistence by his ready pen.
"Thus," he continued, "pass'd unvaried years,
"Without events producing hopes or fears."
Augmented pay procured him decent wealth,

But years advancing undermined his health;
Then oft-times in delightful dream he flew
To England's shore, and scenes his childhood knew:
He saw his parents, saw his fav'rite maid,   420
No feature wrinkled, not a charm decay'd;
And thus excited, in his bosom rose
A wish so strong, it baffled his repose;
Anxious he felt on English earth to lie;
To view his native soil, and there to die.
    He then described the gloom, the dread he found,
When first he landed on the chosen ground,
Where undefined was all he hoped and fear'd,
And how confused and troubled all appear'd;
His thoughts in past and present scenes employ'd,   430
All views in future blighted and destroy'd:
His were a medley of bewild'ring themes,
Sad as realities, and wild as dreams.
    Here his relation closes, but his mind
Flies back again some resting-place to find;
Thus silent, musing through the day, he sees
His children sporting by those lofty trees,
Their mother singing in the shady scene,
Where the fresh springs burst o'er the lively green; –
So strong his eager fancy, he affrights   440
The faithful widow by its powerful flights;
For what disturbs him he aloud will tell,
And cry – "'Tis she, my wife! my Isabel!
"Where are my children?" – Judith grieves to hear
How the soul works in sorrows so severe;
Assiduous all his wishes to attend,
Deprived of much, he yet may boast a friend;
Watch'd by her care, in sleep, his spirit takes
Its flight, and watchful finds her when he wakes.
    'Tis now her office; her attention see!   450
While her friend sleeps beneath that shading tree,
Careful she guards him from the glowing heat,

113

And pensive muses at her Allen's feet.
    And where is he? Ah! doubtless in those scenes
Of his best days, amid the vivid greens,
Fresh with unnumber'd rills, where ev'ry gale
Breathes the rich fragrance of the neighb'ring vale;
Smiles not his wife, and listens as there comes
The night-bird's music from the thick'ning glooms?
And as he sits with all these treasures nigh,   460
Blaze not with fairy light the phosphor-fly,
When like a sparkling gem it wheels illumined by?
This is the joy that now so plainly speaks
In the warm transient flushing of his cheeks;
For he is list'ning to the fancied noise
Of his own children, eager in their joys:
All this he feels, a dream's delusive bliss
Gives the expression, and the glow like this.
And now his Judith lays her knitting by,
These strong emotions in her friend to spy;   470
For she can fully of their nature deem –
But see! he breaks the long-protracted theme,
And wakes and cries – "My God! 'twas but a dream."

The Frank Courtship

Grave Jonas Kindred, Sybil Kindred's sire,
Was six feet high, and look'd six inches higher;
Erect, morose, determined, solemn, slow,
Who knew the man, could never cease to know;
His faithful spouse, when Jonas was not by,
Had a firm presence and a steady eye;
But with her husband dropp'd her look and tone,
And Jonas ruled unquestion'd and alone.
    He read, and oft would quote the sacred words,
How pious husbands of their wives were lords;   10

Sarah called Abraham lord! and who could be,
So Jonas thought, a greater man than he?
Himself he view'd with undisguised respect,
And never pardon'd freedom or neglect.

They had one daughter, and this favourite child
Had oft the father of his spleen beguiled;
Soothed by attention from her early years,
She gain'd all wishes by her smiles or tears:
But Sybil then was in that playful time,
When contradiction is not held a crime;   20
When parents yield their children idle praise
For faults corrected in their after days.

Peace in the sober house of Jonas dwelt,
Where each his duty and his station felt:
Yet not that peace some favour'd mortals find,
In equal views and harmony of mind;
Not the soft peace that blesses those who love,
Where all with one consent in union move;
But it was that which one superior will
Commands, by making all inferiors still;   30
Who bids all murmurs, all objections cease,
And with imperious voice announces – Peace!

They were, to wit, a remnant of that crew
Who, as their foes maintain, their sovereign slew;
An independent race, precise, correct,
Who ever married in the kindred sect:
No son or daughter of their order wed
A friend to England's king who lost his head;
Cromwell was still their saint, and when they met,
They mourn'd that saints were not our rulers yet.   40

Fix'd were their habits; they arose betimes,
Then pray'd their hour, and sang their party-rhymes:
Their meals were plenteous, regular, and plain;
The trade of Jonas brought him constant gain;
Vender of hops and malt, of coals and corn –
And, like his father, he was merchant born:

Neat was their house; each table, chair, and stool,
Stood in its place, or moving moved by rule;
No lively print or picture graced the room;
A plain brown paper lent its decent gloom;   50
But here the eye, in glancing round, survey'd
A small recess that seem'd for china made;
Such pleasing pictures seem'd this pencill'd ware,
That few would search for nobler objects there –
Yet, turn'd by chosen friends, and there appear'd
His stern, strong features, whom they all revered;
For there in lofty air was seen to stand
The bold protector of the conquer'd land;
Drawn in that look with which he wept and swore,
Turn'd out the members, and made fast the door,   60
Ridding the house of every knave and drone,
Forced, though it grieved his soul, to rule alone.
The stern still smile each friend approving gave,
Then turn'd the view, and all again were grave.
    There stood a clock, though small the owner's need,
For habit told when all things should proceed;
Few their amusements, but when friends appear'd,
They with the world's distress their spirits cheer'd;
The nation's guilt, that would not long endure
The reign of men so modest and so pure: 70
Their town was large, and seldom pass'd a day
But some had fail'd, and others gone astray;
Clerks had absconded, wives eloped, girls flown
To Gretna-Green, or sons rebellious grown;
Quarrels and fires arose; – and it was plain
The times were bad; the saints had ceased to reign!
A few yet lived to languish and to mourn
For good old manners never to return.
    Jonas had sisters, and of these was one
Who lost a husband and an only son: 80
Twelve months her sables she in sorrow wore,
And mourn'd so long that she could mourn no more.

116

Distant from Jonas, and from all her race,
She now resided in a lively place;
There, by the sect unseen, at whist she play'd,
Nor was of churchmen or their church afraid:
If much of this the graver brother heard,
He something censured, but he little fear'd;
He knew her rich and frugal; for the rest,
He felt no care, or, if he felt, suppress'd: 90
Nor for companion when she ask'd her niece,
Had he suspicions that disturb'd his peace;
Frugal and rich, these virtues as a charm
Preserved the thoughtful man from all alarm;
An infant yet, she soon would home return,
Nor stay the manners of the world to learn;
Meantime his boys would all his care engross,
And be his comforts if he felt the loss.

The sprightly Sybil, pleased and unconfined,
Felt the pure pleasure of the op'ning mind: 100
All here was gay and cheerful – all at home
Unvaried quiet and unruffled gloom:
There were no changes, and amusements few;
Here, all was varied, wonderful, and new;
There were plain meals, plain dresses, and grave looks –
Here, gay companions and amusing books;
And the young beauty soon began to taste
The light vocations of the scene she graced.

A man of business feels it as a crime
On calls domestic to consume his time; 110
Yet this grave man had not so cold a heart,
But with his daughter he was grieved to part:
And he demanded that in every year
The aunt and niece should at his house appear.

"Yes! we must go, my child, and by our dress
"A grave conformity of mind express;
"Must sing at meeting, and from cards refrain,
"The more t'enjoy when we return again."

117

Thus spake the aunt, and the discerning child
Was pleased to learn how fathers are beguiled.   120
Her artful part the young dissembler took,
And from the matron caught th'approving look:
When thrice the friends had met, excuse was sent
For more delay, and Jonas was content;
Till a tall maiden by her sire was seen,
In all the bloom and beauty of sixteen;
He gazed admiring; – she, with visage prim,
Glanced an arch look of gravity on him;
For she was gay at heart, but wore disguise,
And stood a vestal in her father's eyes: 130
Pure, pensive, simple, sad; the damsel's heart,
When Jonas praised, reproved her for the part;
For Sybil, fond of pleasure, gay and light,
Had still a secret bias to the right;
Vain as she was – and flattery made her vain –
Her simulation gave her bosom pain.

Again return'd, the matron and the niece
Found the late quiet gave their joy increase;
The aunt infirm, no more her visits paid,
But still with her sojourn'd the favourite maid.   140
Letters were sent when franks could be procured,
And when they could not, silence was endured;
All were in health, and if they older grew,
It seem'd a fact that none among them knew;
The aunt and niece still led a pleasant life,
And quiet days had Jonas and his wife.

Near him a widow dwelt of worthy fame,
Like his her manners, and her creed the same;
The wealth her husband left, her care retain'd
For one tall youth, and widow she remain'd;   150
His love respectful all her care repaid,
Her wishes watch'd, and her commands obey'd.

Sober he was and grave from early youth,
Mindful of forms, but more intent on truth;

118

In a light drab he uniformly dress'd,
And look serene th'unruffled mind express'd;
A hat with ample verge his brows o'erspread,
And his brown locks curl'd graceful on his head;
Yet might observers in his speaking eye
Some observation, some acuteness spy;   160
The friendly thought it keen, the treacherous deem'd it sly;
Yet not a crime could foe or friend detect,
His actions all were, like his speech, correct;
And they who jested on a mind so sound,
Upon his virtues must their laughter found;
Chaste, sober, solemn, and devout they named
Him who was thus, and not of *this* ashamed.
    Such were the virtues Jonas found in one
In whom he warmly wish'd to find a son:
Three years had pass'd since he had Sybil seen;   170
But she was doubtless what she once had been,
Lovely and mild, obedient and discreet;
The pair must love whenever they should meet;
Then ere the widow or her son should choose
Some happier maid, he would explain his views;
Now she, like him, was politic and shrewd,
With strong desire of lawful gain embued;
To all he said, she bow'd with much respect,
Pleased to comply, yet seeming to reject;
Cool and yet eager, each admired the strength   180
Of the opponent, and agreed at length:
As a drawn battle shows to each a force,
Powerful as his, he honours it of course;
So in these neighbours, each the power discern'd,
And gave the praise that was to each return'd.
    Jonas now ask'd his daughter – and the aunt,
Though loth to lose her, was obliged to grant: –
But would not Sybil to the matron cling,
And fear to leave the shelter of her wing?
No! in the young there lives a love of change,   190

119

And to the easy they prefer the strange!
Then too the joys she once pursued with zeal,
From whist and visits sprung, she ceased to feel;
When with the matrons Sybil first sat down,
To cut for partners and to stake her crown,
This to the youthful maid preferment seem'd,
Who thought what woman she was then esteem'd;
But in few years, when she perceived, indeed,
The real woman to the girl succeed,
No longer tricks and honours fill'd her mind,   200
But other feelings, not so well defined;
She then reluctant grew, and thought it hard,
To sit and ponder o'er an ugly card;
Rather the nut-tree shade the nymph preferr'd,
Pleased with the pensive gloom and evening bird;
Thither, from company retired, she took
The silent walk, or read the fav'rite book.
   The father's letter, sudden, short, and kind,
Awaked her wonder, and disturb'd her mind;
She found new dreams upon her fancy seize,   210
Wild roving thoughts and endless reveries:
The parting came; – and when the aunt perceived
The tears of Sybil, and how much she grieved –
To love for her that tender grief she laid,
That various, soft, contending passions made.
   When Sybil rested in her father's arms,
His pride exulted in a daughter's charms;
A maid accomplish'd he was pleased to find,
Nor seem'd the form more lovely than the mind:
But when the fit of pride and fondness fled,   220
He saw his judgment by his hopes misled;
High were the lady's spirits, far more free
Her mode of speaking than a maid's should be;
Too much, as Jonas thought, she seem'd to know,
And all her knowledge was disposed to show;
"Too gay her dress, like theirs who idly dote

"On a young coxcomb, or a coxcomb's coat;
"In foolish spirits when our friends appear,
"And vainly grave when not a man is near."
 Thus Jonas, adding to his sorrow blame,   230
And terms disdainful to his sister's name: –
"The sinful wretch has by her arts defiled
"The ductile spirit of my darling child."
 "The maid is virtuous," said the dame – Quoth he,
"Let her give proof, by acting virtuously:
"Is it in gaping when the elders pray?
"In reading nonsense half a summer's day?
"In those mock forms that she delights to trace,
"Or her loud laughs in Hezekiah's face?
"She – O Susannah! – to the world belongs;   240
"She loves the follies of its idle throngs,
"And reads soft tales of love, and sings love's soft'ning songs.
"But, as our friend is yet delay'd in town,
"We must prepare her till the youth comes down;
"You shall advise the maiden; I will threat;
"Her fears and hopes may yield us comfort yet."
 Now the grave father took the lass aside,
Demanding sternly, "Wilt thou be a bride?"
She answer'd, calling up an air sedate,
"I have not vow'd against the holy state."   250
 "No folly, Sybil," said the parent; "know
"What to their parents virtuous maidens owe:
"A worthy, wealthy youth, whom I approve,
"Must thou prepare to honour and to love.
"Formal to thee his air and dress may seem,
"But the good youth is worthy of esteem;
"Shouldst thou with rudeness treat him; of disdain
"Should he with justice or of slight complain,
"Or of one taunting speech give certain proof,
"Girl! I reject thee from my sober roof."   260
 "My aunt," said Sybil, "will with pride protect
"One whom a father can for this reject;

121

"Nor shall a formal, rigid, soul-less boy
"My manners alter, or my views destroy!"
  Jonas then lifted up his hands on high,
And utt'ring something 'twixt a groan and sigh,
Left the determined maid, her doubtful mother by.
  "Hear me," she said; "incline thy heart, my child,
"And fix thy fancy on a man so mild:
"Thy father, Sybil, never could be moved   270
"By one who loved him, or by one he loved.
"Union like ours is but a bargain made
"By slave and tyrant – he will be obey'd;
"Then calls the quiet, comfort – but thy youth
"Is mild by nature, and as frank as truth."
  "But will he love?" said Sybil; "I am told
"That these mild creatures are by nature cold."
  "Alas!" the matron answer'd, "much I dread
"That dangerous love by which the young are led!
"That love is earthy; you the creature prize,   280
"And trust your feelings and believe your eyes:
"Can eyes and feelings inward worth descry?
"No! my fair daughter, on our choice rely!
"Your love, like that display'd upon the stage,
"Indulged is folly, and opposed is rage; –
"More prudent love our sober couples show,
"All that to mortal beings, mortals owe;
"All flesh is grass – before you give a heart,
"Remember, Sybil, that in death you part;
"And should your husband die before your love,   290
"What needless anguish must a widow prove!
"No! my fair child, let all such visions cease;
"Yield but esteem, and only try for peace."
  "I must be loved," said Sybil; "I must see
"The man in terrors who aspires to me;
"At my forbidding frown, his heart must ache,
"His tongue must falter, and his frame must shake:
"And if I grant him at my feet to kneel,

"What trembling, fearful pleasure he must feel;
"Nay, such the raptures that my smiles inspire,   300
"That reason's self must for a time retire."
   "Alas! for good Josiah," said the dame,
"These wicked thoughts would fill his soul with shame;
"He kneel and tremble at a thing of dust!
"He cannot, child:" – the child replied, "He must."
   They ceased: the matron left her with a frown;
So Jonas met her when the youth came down:
"Behold," said he, "thy future spouse attends;
"Receive him, daughter, as the best of friends;
"Observe, respect him – humble be each word,   310
"That welcomes home thy husband and thy lord."
   Forewarn'd, thought Sybil, with a bitter smile,
I shall prepare my manner and my style.
   Ere yet Josiah enter'd on his task,
The father met him – "Deign to wear a mask
"A few dull days, Josiah – but a few –
"It is our duty, and the sex's due;
"I wore it once, and every grateful wife
"Repays it with obedience through her life:
"Have no regard to Sybil's dress, have none   320
"To her pert language, to her flippant tone:
"Henceforward thou shalt rule unquestion'd and alone;
"And she thy pleasure in thy looks shall seek –
"How she shall dress, and whether she may speak."
   A sober smile return'd the youth, and said,
"Can I cause fear, who am myself afraid?"
   Sybil, meantime, sat thoughtful in her room,
And often wonder'd – "Will the creature come?
"Nothing shall tempt, shall force me to bestow
"My hand upon him – yet I wish to know."   330
   The door unclosed, and she beheld her sire
Lead in the youth, then hasten to retire;
"Daughter, my friend – my daughter, friend" – he cried,
And gave a meaning look, and stepp'd aside;

That look contain'd a mingled threat and prayer,
"Do take him, child – offend him, if you dare."
  The couple gazed – were silent, and the maid
Look'd in his face, to make the man afraid;
The man, unmoved, upon the maiden cast
A steady view – so salutation pass'd: 340
But in this instant Sybil's eye had seen
The tall fair person, and the still staid mien;
The glow that temp'rance o'er the cheek had spread,
Where the soft down half veil'd the purest red;
And the serene deportment that proclaim'd
A heart unspotted, and a life unblamed:
But then with these she saw attire too plain,
The pale brown coat, though worn without a stain;
The formal air, and something of the pride
That indicates the wealth it seems to hide;   350
And looks that were not, she conceived, exempt
From a proud pity, or a sly contempt.
  Josiah's eyes had their employment too,
Engaged and soften'd by so bright a view;
A fair and meaning face, an eye of fire,
That check'd the bold, and made the free retire:
But then with these he mark'd the studied dress
And lofty air, that scorn or pride express;
With that insidious look, that seem'd to hide
In an affected smile the scorn and pride;   360
And if his mind the virgin's meaning caught,
He saw a foe with treacherous purpose fraught –
Captive the heart to take, and to reject it caught.
  Silent they sate – thought Sybil, that he seeks
Something, no doubt; I wonder if he speaks:
Scarcely she wonder'd, when these accents fell
Slow in her ear – "Fair maiden, art thou well?"
"Art thou physician?" she replied; "my hand,
"My pulse, at least, shall be at thy command."
  She said – and saw, surprised, Josiah kneel,   370

And gave his lips the offer'd pulse to feel;
The rosy colour rising in her cheek,
Seem'd that surprise unmix'd with wrath to speak;
Then sternness she assumed, and – "Doctor, tell,
"Thy words cannot alarm me – am I well?"
    "Thou art," said he; "and yet thy dress so light,
"I do conceive, some danger must excite:"
"In whom?" said Sybil, with a look demure:
"In more," said he, "than I expect to cure.
"I, in thy light luxuriant robe, behold   380
"Want and excess, abounding and yet cold;
"Here needed, there display'd, in many a wanton fold:
"Both health and beauty, learned authors show,
"From a just medium in our clothing flow."
    "Proceed, good doctor; if so great my need,
"What is thy fee? Good doctor! pray proceed."
    "Large is my fee, fair lady, but I take
"None till some progress in my cure I make:
"Thou hast disease, fair maiden; thou art vain;
"Within that face sit insult and disdain;   390
"Thou art enamour'd of thyself; my art
"Can see the naughty malice of thy heart:
"With a strong pleasure would thy bosom move,
"Were I to own thy power, and ask thy love;
"And such thy beauty, damsel, that I might,
"But for thy pride, feel danger in thy sight,
"And lose my present peace in dreams of vain delight."
    "And can thy patients," said the nymph, "endure
"Physic like this? and will it work a cure?"
    "Such is my hope, fair damsel; thou, I find,   400
"Hast the true tokens of a noble mind;
"But the world wins thee, Sybil, and thy joys
"Are placed in trifles, fashions, follies, toys;
"Thou hast sought pleasure in the world around,
"That in thine own pure bosom should be found:
"Did all that world admire thee, praise and love,

125

"Could it the least of nature's pains remove?
"Could it for errors, follies, sins atone,
"Or give thee comfort, thoughtful and alone?
"It has, believe me, maid, no power to charm   410
"Thy soul from sorrow, or thy flesh from harm:
"Turn then, fair creature, from a world of sin,
"And seek the jewel happiness within."
    "Speak'st thou at meeting?" said the nymph; "thy speech
"Is that of mortal very prone to teach;
"But wouldst thou, doctor, from the patient learn
"Thine own disease? – The cure is thy concern."
    "Yea, with good will." – "Then know, 'tis thy complaint,
"That, for a sinner, thou'rt too much a saint;
"Hast too much show of the sedate and pure,   420
"And without cause art formal and demure:
"This makes a man unsocial, unpolite;
"Odious when wrong, and insolent if right.
"Thou may'st be good, but why should goodness be
"Wrapt in a garb of such formality?
"Thy person well might please a damsel's eye,
"In decent habit with a scarlet dye;
"But, jest apart – what virtue canst thou trace
"In that broad brim that hides thy sober face?
"Does that long-skirted drab, that over-nice   430
"And formal clothing, prove a scorn of vice?
"Then for thine accent – what in sound can be
"So void of grace as dull monotony?
"Love has a thousand varied notes to move
"The human heart; – thou may'st not speak of love
"Till thou hast cast thy formal ways aside,
"And those becoming youth and nature tried:
"Not till exterior freedom, spirit, ease,
"Prove it thy study and delight to please;
"Not till these follies meet thy just disdain,   440
"While yet thy virtues and thy worth remain."
    "This is severe! – Oh! maiden, wilt not thou
126

"Something for habits, manners, modes, allow?" –
"Yes! but allowing much, I much require,
"In my behalf, for manners, modes, attire!"
    "True, lovely Sybil; and, this point agreed,
"Let me to those of greater weight proceed:
"Thy father!" – "Nay," she quickly interposed,
"Good doctor, here our conference is closed!"
    Then left the youth, who, lost in his retreat,   450
Pass'd the good matron on her garden-seat;
His looks were troubled, and his air, once mild
And calm, was hurried: – "My audacious child!"
Exclaim'd the dame, "I read what she has done
"In thy displeasure – Ah! the thoughtless one;
"But yet, Josiah, to my stern good man
"Speak of the maid as mildly as you can:
"Can you not seem to woo a little while
"The daughter's will, the father to beguile?
"So that his wrath in time may wear away;   460
"Will you preserve our peace, Josiah? say."
    "Yes! my good neighbour," said the gentle youth,
"Rely securely on my care and truth;
"And should thy comfort with my efforts cease,
"And only then – perpetual is thy peace."
    The dame had doubts: she well his virtues knew,
His deeds were friendly, and his words were true;
"But to address this vixen is a task
"He is ashamed to take, and I to ask."
Soon as the father from Josiah learn'd   470
What pass'd with Sybil, he the truth discern'd.
"He loves," the man exclaim'd, "he loves, 'tis plain,
"The thoughtless girl, and shall he love in vain?
"She may be stubborn, but she shall be tried,
"Born as she is of wilfulness and pride."
    With anger fraught, but willing to persuade,
The wrathful father met the smiling maid:
"Sybil," said he, "I long, and yet I dread
127

"To know thy conduct – hath Josiah fled?
"And, grieved and fretted by thy scornful air,   480
"For his lost peace betaken him to prayer?
"Couldst thou his pure and modest mind distress,
"By vile remarks upon his speech, address,
"Attire, and voice?" – "All this I must confess." –
"Unhappy child! what labour will it cost
"To win him back!" – "I do not think him lost."
"Courts he then, trifler! insult and disdain?" –
"No: but from these he courts me to refrain."
"Then hear me, Sybil – should Josiah leave
"Thy father's house?" – "My father's child would grieve:"   490
"That is of grace, and if he come again
"To speak of love?" – "I might from grief refrain." –
"Then wilt thou, daughter, our design embrace?" –
"Can I resist it, if it be of grace?"
"Dear child! in three plain words thy mind express –
"Wilt thou have this good youth?" "Dear father! yes."

The Widow's Tale

To farmer Moss, in Langar Vale, came down
His only daughter, from her school in town;
A tender, timid maid! who knew not how
To pass a pig-sty, or to face a cow:
Smiling she came, with petty talents graced,
A fair complexion, and a slender waist.

   Used to spare meals, disposed in manner pure,
Her father's kitchen she could ill endure;
Where by the steaming beef he hungry sat,
And laid at once a pound upon his plate;   10
Hot from the field, her eager brother seized
An equal part, and hunger's rage appeased;
The air, surcharged with moisture, flagg'd around,

128

And the offended damsel sigh'd and frown'd;
The swelling fat in lumps conglomerate laid,
And fancy's sickness seized the loathing maid:
But when the men beside their station took,
The maidens with them, and with these the cook;
When one huge wooden bowl before them stood,
Fill'd with huge balls of farinaceous food;   20
With bacon, mass saline, where never lean
Beneath the brown and bristly rind was seen;
When from a single horn the party drew
Their copious draughts of heavy ale and new;
When the coarse cloth she saw, with many a stain,
Soil'd by rude hinds who cut and came again –
She could not breathe; but, with a heavy sigh,
Rein'd the fair neck, and shut th'offended eye;
She minced the sanguine flesh in frustums fine,
And wonder'd much to see the creatures dine: 30
When she resolved her father's heart to move,
If hearts of farmers were alive to love.
    She now entreated by herself to sit
In the small parlour, if papa thought fit,
And there to dine, to read, to work alone: –
"No!" said the farmer, in an angry tone;
"These are your school-taught airs; your mother's pride
"Would send you there; but I am now your guide. –
"Arise betimes, our early meal prepare,
"And this despatch'd, let business be your care;   40
"Look to the lasses, let there be not one
"Who lacks attention, till her tasks be done;
"In every household work your portion take,
"And what you make not, see that others make:
"At leisure times attend the wheel, and see
"The whit'ning web be sprinkled on the Lea;
"When thus employ'd, should our young neighbour view
"An useful lass, you may have more to do."
    Dreadful were these commands; but worse than these

129

The parting hint – a farmer could not please: 50
'Tis true she had without abhorrence seen
Young Harry Carr, when he was smart and clean;
But to be married – be a farmer's wife –
A slave! a drudge! – she could not, for her life.

　　With swimming eyes the fretful nymph withdrew,
And, deeply sighing, to her chamber flew;
There on her knees, to Heav'n she grieving pray'd
For change of prospect to a tortured maid.

　　Harry, a youth whose late-departed sire
Had left him all industrious men require,   60
Saw the pale beauty – and her shape and air
Engaged him much, and yet he must forbear:
"For my small farm what can the damsel do?"
He said – then stopp'd to take another view:
"Pity so sweet a lass will nothing learn
"Of household cares – for what can beauty earn
"By those small arts which they at school attain,
"That keep them useless, and yet make them vain?"

　　This luckless damsel look'd the village round,
To find a friend, and one was quickly found;   70
A pensive widow – whose mild air and dress
Pleased the sad nymph, who wish'd her soul's distress
To one so seeming kind, confiding, to confess. –

　　"What lady that?" the anxious lass inquired,
Who then beheld the one she most admired:
"Here," said the brother, "are no ladies seen –
"That is a widow dwelling on the green;
"A dainty dame, who can but barely live
"On her poor pittance, yet contrives to give;
"She happier days has known, but seems at ease,   80
"And you may call her lady, if you please:
"But if you wish, good sister, to improve,
"You shall see twenty better worth your love."

　　These Nancy met; but, spite of all they taught,
This useless widow was the one she sought:

The father growl'd; but said he knew no harm
In such connexion that could give alarm;
"And if we thwart the trifler in her course,
"'Tis odds against us she will take a worse."
   Then met the friends: the widow heard the sigh   90
That ask'd at once compassion and reply: –
"Would you, my child, converse with one so poor,
"Yours were the kindness – yonder is my door;
"And, save the time that we in public pray,
"From that poor cottage I but rarely stray."
   There went the nymph, and made her strong complaints,
Painting her wo as injured feeling paints.
   "Oh, dearest friend! do think how one must feel,
"Shock'd all day long, and sicken'd every meal;
"Could you behold our kitchen (and to you   100
"A scene so shocking must indeed be new),
"A mind like yours, with true refinement graced,
"Would let no vulgar scenes pollute your taste;
"And yet, in truth, from such a polish'd mind
"All base ideas must resistance find,
"And sordid pictures from the fancy pass,
"As the breath startles from the polish'd glass.
   "Here you enjoy a sweet romantic scene,
"Without so pleasant, and within so clean;
"These twining jess'mines, what delicious gloom   110
"And soothing fragrance yield they to the room!
"What lovely garden! there you oft retire,
"And tales of wo and tenderness admire:
"In that neat case your books, in order placed,
"Soothe the full soul, and charm the cultured taste;
"And thus, while all about you wears a charm,
"How must you scorn the farmer and the farm!"
   The widow smiled, and "Know you not," said she,
"How much these farmers scorn or pity me;
"Who see what you admire, and laugh at all they see?   120
"True, their opinion alters not my fate,

"By falsely judging of an humble state:
"This garden, you with such delight behold,
"Tempts not a feeble dame who dreads the cold;
"These plants, which please so well your livelier sense,
"To mine but little of their sweets dispense;
"Books soon are painful to my failing sight,
"And oftener read from duty than delight;
"(Yet let me own, that I can sometimes find
"Both joy and duty in the act combined;)   130
"But view me rightly, you will see no more
"Than a poor female, willing to be poor;
"Happy indeed, but not in books nor flowers,
"Not in fair dreams, indulged in earlier hours,
"Of never-tasted joys; – such visions shun,
"My youthful friend, nor scorn the farmer's son."
    "Nay," said the damsel, nothing pleased to see
A friend's advice could like a father's be,
"Bless'd in your cottage, you must surely smile
"At those who live in our detested style: 140
"To my Lucinda's sympathizing heart
"Could I my prospects and my griefs impart,
"She would console me; but I dare not show
"Ills that would wound her tender soul to know:
"And I confess, it shocks my pride to tell
"The secrets of the prison where I dwell;
"For that dear maiden would be shock'd to feel
"The secrets I should shudder to reveal;
"When told her friend was by a parent ask'd,
"Fed you the swine? – Good heav'n! how I am task'd!   150
"What! can you smile? Ah! smile not at the grief
"That woos your pity and demands relief."
    "Trifles, my love; you take a false alarm;
"Think, I beseech you, better of the farm:
"Duties in every state demand your care,
"And light are those that will require it there:
"Fix on the youth a favouring eye, and these,

"To him pertaining, or as his, will please."
    "What words," the lass replied, "offend my ear!
"Try you my patience? Can you be sincere?   160
"And am I told a willing hand to give
"To a rude farmer, and with rustic live?
"Far other fate was yours: – some gentle youth
"Admired your beauty, and avow'd his truth;
"The power of love prevail'd, and freely both
"Gave the fond heart, and pledged the binding oath;
"And then the rivals' plot, the parent's power,
"And jealous fears, drew on the happy hour:
"Ah! let not memory lose the blissful view,
"But fairly show what love has done for you."   170
    "Agreed, my daughter; what my heart has known
"Of love's strange power shall be with frankness shown:
"But let me warn you, that experience finds
"Few of the scenes that lively hope designs." –
    "Mysterious all," said Nancy; "you, I know,
"Have suffer'd much; now deign the grief to show; –
"I am your friend, and so prepare my heart
"In all your sorrows to receive a part."
    The widow answer'd: "I had once, like you,
"Such thoughts of love; no dream is more untrue: 180
"You judge it fated and decreed to dwell
"In youthful hearts, which nothing can expel,
"A passion doom'd to reign, and irresistible.
"The struggling mind, when once subdued, in vain
"Rejects the fury or defies the pain;
"The strongest reason fails the flame t'allay,
"And resolution droops and faints away:
"Hence, when the destined lovers meet, they prove
"At once the force of this all-powerful love;
"Each from that period feels the mutual smart,   190
"Nor seeks to cure it – heart is changed for heart;
"Nor is there peace till they delighted stand,
"And, at the altar – hand is join'd to hand.

133

"Alas! my child, there are who, dreaming so,
"Waste their fresh youth, and waking feel the wo;
"There is no spirit sent the heart to move
"With such prevailing and alarming love;
"Passion to reason will submit – or why
"Should wealthy maids the poorest swains deny?
"Or how could classes and degrees create   200
"The slightest bar to such resistless fate?
"Yet high and low, you see, forbear to mix;
"No beggars' eyes the heart of kings transfix;
"And who but am'rous peers or nobles sigh
"When titled beauties pass triumphant by?
"For reason wakes, proud wishes to reprove;
"You cannot hope, and therefore dare not love:
"All would be safe, did we at first inquire –
"'Does reason sanction what our hearts desire?'
"But quitting precept, let example show   210
"What joys from love uncheck'd by prudence flow.
    "A youth my father in his office placed,
"Of humble fortune, but with sense and taste;
"But he was thin and pale, had downcast looks;
"He studied much, and pored upon his books:
"Confused he was when seen, and, when he saw
"Me or my sisters, would in haste withdraw;
"And had this youth departed with the year,
"His loss had cost us neither sigh nor tear.
    "But with my father still the youth remain'd,   220
"And more reward and kinder notice gain'd:
"He often, reading, to the garden stray'd,
"Where I by books or musing was delay'd;
"This to discourse in summer evenings led,
"Of these same evenings, or of what we read:
"On such occasions we were much alone;
"But, save the look, the manner, and the tone,
"(These might have meaning), all that we discuss'd
"We could with pleasure to a parent trust.

134

"At length 'twas friendship – and my friend and I   230
"Said we were happy, and began to sigh:
"My sisters first, and then my father, found
"That we were wandering o'er enchanted ground;
"But he had troubles in his own affairs,
"And would not bear addition to his cares:
"With pity moved, yet angry, 'Child,' said he,
"'Will you embrace contempt and beggary?
"'Can you endure to see each other cursed
"'By want, of every human wo the worst?
"'Warring for ever with distress, in dread   240
"'Either of begging or of wanting bread;
"'While poverty, with unrelenting force,
"'Will your own offspring from your love divorce;
"'They, through your folly, must be doom'd to pine,
"'And you deplore your passion, or resign;
"'For, if it die, what good will then remain?
"'And if it live, it doubles every pain.'"
   "But you were true," exclaim'd the lass, "and fled
"The tyrant's power who fill'd your soul with dread?"
"But," said the smiling friend, "he fill'd my mouth with   250
       bread:
"And in what other place that bread to gain
"We long consider'd, and we sought in vain;
"This was my twentieth year – at thirty-five
"Our hope was fainter, yet our love alive;
"So many years in anxious doubt had pass'd."
"Then," said the damsel, "you were bless'd at last?"
A smile again adorn'd the widow's face,
But soon a starting tear usurp'd its place.
   "Slow pass'd the heavy years, and each had more
"Pains and vexations than the years before.   260
"My father fail'd; his family was rent,
"And to new states his grieving daughters sent;
"Each to more thriving kindred found a way,
"Guests without welcome – servants without pay;
135

"Our parting hour was grievous; still I feel
"The sad, sweet converse at our final meal;
"Our father then reveal'd his former fears,
"Cause of his sternness, and then join'd our tears;
"Kindly he strove our feelings to repress,
"But died, and left us heirs to his distress.   270
"The rich, as humble friends, my sisters chose,
"I with a wealthy widow sought repose;
"Who with a chilling frown her friend received,
"Bade me rejoice, and wonder'd that I grieved:
"In vain my anxious lover tried his skill
"To rise in life, he was dependent still;
"We met in grief, nor can I paint the fears
"Of these unhappy, troubled, trying years:
"Our dying hopes and stronger fears between,
"We felt no season peaceful or serene;   280
"Our fleeting joys, like meteors in the night,
"Shone on our gloom with inauspicious light;
"And then domestic sorrows, till the mind,
"Worn with distresses, to despair inclined;
"Add to the ill that from the passion flows,
"When its contemptuous frown the world bestows,
"The peevish spirit caused by long delay,
"When being gloomy we contemn the gay,
"When, being wretched, we incline to hate
"And censure others in a happier state;   290
"Yet loving still, and still compell'd to move
"In the sad labyrinth of ling'ring love:
"While you, exempt from want, despair, alarm,
"May wed – oh! take the farmer and the farm."
    "Nay," said the nymph, "joy smiled on you at last?"
"Smiled for a moment," she replied, "and pass'd:
"My lover still the same dull means pursued,
"Assistant call'd, but kept in servitude;
"His spirits wearied in the prime of life,
"By fears and wishes in eternal strife;   300

"At length he urged impatient – 'Now consent;
"'With thee united, fortune may relent.'
"I paused, consenting; but a friend arose,
"Pleased a fair view, though distant, to disclose;
"From the rough ocean we beheld a gleam
"Of joy, as transient as the joys we dream;
"By lying hopes deceived, my friend retired,
"And sail'd – was wounded – reach'd us – and expired!
"You shall behold his grave, and when I die,
"There – but 'tis folly – I request to lie."   310
    "Thus," said the lass, "to joy you bade adieu!
"But how a widow? – that cannot be true:
"Or was it force, in some unhappy hour,
"That placed you, grieving, in a tyrant's power?"
    "Force, my young friend, when forty years are fled,
"Is what a woman seldom has to dread;
"She needs no brazen locks nor guarding walls,
"And seldom comes a lover though she calls:
"Yet moved by fancy, one approved my face,
"Though time and tears had wrought it much disgrace.   320
    "The man I married was sedate and meek,
"And spoke of love as men in earnest speak;
"Poor as I was, he ceaseless sought, for years,
"A heart in sorrow and a face in tears;
"That heart I gave not; and 'twas long before
"I gave attention, and then nothing more;
"But in my breast some grateful feeling rose
"For one whose love so sad a subject chose;
"Till long delaying, fearing to repent,
"But grateful still, I gave a cold assent.   330
    "Thus we were wed; no fault had I to find,
"And he but one; my heart could not be kind:
"Alas! of every early hope bereft,
"There was no fondness in my bosom left;
"So had I told him, but had told in vain,
"He lived but to indulge me and complain:

137

"His was this cottage, he inclosed this ground,
"And planted all these blooming shrubs around;
"He to my room these curious trifles brought,
"And with assiduous love my pleasure sought;   340
"He lived to please me, and I ofttimes strove
"Smiling, to thank his unrequited love:
"'Teach me,' he cried, 'that pensive mind to ease,
"'For all my pleasure is the hope to please.'

    "Serene, though heavy, were the days we spent,
"Yet kind each word, and gen'rous each intent;
"But his dejection lessen'd every day,
"And to a placid kindness died away:
"In tranquil ease we pass'd our latter years,
"By griefs untroubled, unassail'd by fears.   350

    "Let not romantic views your bosom sway,
"Yield to your duties, and their call obey:
"Fly not a youth, frank, honest, and sincere;
"Observe his merits, and his passion hear!
"'Tis true, no hero, but a farmer sues —
"Slow in his speech, but worthy in his views;
"With him you cannot that affliction prove,
"That rends the bosom of the poor in love:
"Health, comfort, competence, and cheerful days,
"Your friends' approval, and your father's praise,   360
"Will crown the deed, and you escape *their* fate
"Who plan so wildly, and are wise too late."

    The damsel heard; at first th'advice was strange,
Yet wrought a happy, nay, a speedy change:
"I have no care," she said, when next they met,
"But one may wonder he is silent yet;
"He looks around him with his usual stare,
"And utters nothing — not that I shall care."

    This pettish humour pleased th'experienced friend —
None need despair, whose silence can offend;   370
"Should I," resumed the thoughtful lass, "consent
"To hear the man, the man may now repent:

138

"Think you my sighs shall call him from the plough,
"Or give one hint, that 'You may woo me now?'"
  "Persist, my love," replied the friend, "and gain
"A parent's praise, *that* cannot be in vain."
  The father saw the change, but not the cause,
And gave the alter'd maid his fond applause:
The coarser manners she in part removed,
In part endured, improving and improved;   380
She spoke of household works, she rose betimes,
And said neglect and indolence were crimes;
The various duties of their life she weigh'd,
And strict attention to her dairy paid;
The names of servants now familiar grew,
And fair Lucinda's from her mind withdrew:
As prudent travellers for their ease assume
Their modes and language to whose lands they come:
So to the farmer this fair lass inclined,
Gave to the business of the farm her mind;   390
To useful arts she turn'd her hand and eye;
And by her manners told him – "You may try."
  Th'observing lover more attention paid,
With growing pleasure, to the alter'd maid;
He fear'd to lose her, and began to see
That a slim beauty might a helpmate be:
'Twixt hope and fear he now the lass address'd,
And in his Sunday robe his love express'd:
She felt no chilling dread, no thrilling joy,
Nor was too quickly kind, too slowly coy;   400
But still she lent an unreluctant ear
To all the rural business of the year;
Till love's strong hopes endured no more delay,
And Harry ask'd, and Nancy named the day.
  "A happy change! my boy," the father cried:
"How lost your sister all her school-day pride?"
The youth replied, "It is the widow's deed:
"The cure is perfect, and was wrought with speed." –

"And comes there, boy, this benefit of books,
"Of that smart dress, and of those dainty looks? 410
"We must be kind – some offerings from the farm
"To the white cot will speak our feelings warm;
"Will show that people, when they know the fact,
"Where they have judged severely, can retract.
"Oft have I smiled, when I beheld her pass
"With cautious step, as if she hurt the grass;
"Where if a snail's retreat she chanced to storm,
"She look'd as begging pardon of the worm;
"And what, said I, still laughing at the view,
"Have these weak creatures in the world to do? 420
"But some are made for action, some to speak;
"And, while she looks so pitiful and meek,
"Her words are weighty, though her nerves are weak."
    Soon told the village-bells the rite was done,
That join'd the school-bred miss and farmer's son;
Her former habits some slight scandal raised,
But real worth was soon perceived and praised;
She, her neat taste imparted to the farm,
And he, th'improving skill and vigorous arm.

The Lover's Journey

It is the soul that sees; the outward eyes
Present the object, but the mind descries;
And thence delight, disgust, or cool indiff'rence rise:
When minds are joyful, then we look around,
And what is seen is all on fairy ground;
Again they sicken, and on every view
Cast their own dull and melancholy hue;
Or, if absorb'd by their peculiar cares,
The vacant eye on viewless matter glares,
Our feelings still upon our views attend, 10

140

And their own natures to the objects lend;
Sorrow and joy are in their influence sure,
Long as the passion reigns th'effects endure;
But love in minds his various changes makes,
And clothes each object with the change he takes;
His light and shade on every view he throws,
And on each object, what he feels, bestows.

Fair was the morning, and the month was June,
When rose a lover; love awakens soon;
Brief his repose, yet much he dreamt the while   20
Of that day's meeting, and his Laura's smile;
Fancy and love that name assign'd to her,
Call'd Susan in the parish-register;
And he no more was John – his Laura gave
The name Orlando to her faithful slave.

Bright shone the glory of the rising day,
When the fond traveller took his favourite way;
He mounted gaily, felt his bosom light,
And all he saw was pleasing in his sight.

"Ye hours of expectation, quickly fly,   30
"And bring on hours of blest reality;
"When I shall Laura see, beside her stand,
"Hear her sweet voice, and press her yielded hand."

First o'er a barren heath beside the coast
Orlando rode, and joy began to boast.

"This neat low gorse," said he, "with golden bloom,
"Delights each sense, is beauty, is perfume;
"And this gay ling, with all its purple flowers,
"A man at leisure might admire for hours;
"This green-fringed cup-moss has a scarlet tip,   40
"That yields to nothing but my Laura's lip;
"And then how fine this herbage! men may say
"A heath is barren; nothing is so gay:
"Barren or bare to call such charming scene
"Argues a mind possess'd by care and spleen."

Onward he went, and fiercer grew the heat,

141

Dust rose in clouds before the horse's feet;
For now he pass'd through lanes of burning sand,
Bounds to thin crops or yet uncultured land;
Where the dark poppy flourish'd on the dry   50
And sterile soil, and mock'd the thin-set rye.
    "How lovely this!" the rapt Orlando said;
"With what delight is labouring man repaid!
"The very lane has sweets that all admire,
"The rambling suckling and the vigorous brier;
"See! wholesome wormwood grows beside the way,
"Where dew-press'd yet the dog-rose bends the spray;
"Fresh herbs the fields, fair shrubs the banks adorn,
"And snow-white bloom falls flaky from the thorn;
"No fostering hand they need, no sheltering wall,   60
"They spring uncultured and they bloom for all."
    The lover rode as hasty lovers ride,
And reach'd a common pasture wild and wide;
Small black-legg'd sheep devour with hunger keen
The meagre herbage, fleshless, lank, and lean;
Such o'er thy level turf, Newmarket! stray,
And there, with other *black-legs* find their prey:
He saw some scatter'd hovels; turf was piled
In square brown stacks; a prospect bleak and wild!
A mill, indeed, was in the centre found,   70
With short sear herbage withering all around;
A smith's black shed opposed a wright's long shop,
And join'd an inn where humble travellers stop.
    "Ay, this is Nature," said the gentle 'squire;
"This ease, peace, pleasure – who would not admire?
"With what delight these sturdy children play,
"And joyful rustics at the close of day;
"Sport follows labour, on this even space
"Will soon commence the wrestling and the race;
"Then will the village-maidens leave their home,   80
"And to the dance with buoyant spirits come;
"No affectation in their looks is seen,

"Nor know they what disguise or flattery mean;
"Nor aught to move an envious pang they see,
"Easy their service, and their love is free;
"Hence early springs that love, it long endures,
"And life's first comfort, while they live, ensures:
"They the low roof and rustic comforts prize,
"Nor cast on prouder mansions envying eyes:
"Sometimes the news at yonder town they hear,   90
"And learn what busier mortals feel and fear;
"Secure themselves, although by tales amazed,
"Of towns bombarded and of cities razed;
"As if they doubted, in their still retreat,
"The very news that makes their quiet sweet,
"And their days happy – happier only knows
"He on whom Laura her regard bestows."
    On rode Orlando, counting all the while
The miles he pass'd and every coming mile;
Like all attracted things, he quicker flies,   100
The place approaching where th'attraction lies;
When next appear'd a *dam* – so call the place –
Where lies a road confined in narrow space;
A work of labour, for on either side
Is level fen, a prospect wild and wide,
With dikes on either hand by ocean's self supplied:
Far on the right the distant sea is seen,
And salt the springs that feed the marsh between;
Beneath an ancient bridge, the straiten'd flood
Rolls through its sloping banks of slimy mud;   110
Near it a sunken boat resists the tide,
That frets and hurries to th'opposing side;
The rushes sharp, that on the borders grow,
Bend their brown flow'rets to the stream below,
Impure in all its course, in all its progress slow:
Here a grave Flora scarcely deigns to bloom,
Nor wears a rosy blush, nor sheds perfume;
The few dull flowers that o'er the place are spread

143

Partake the nature of their fenny bed;
Here on its wiry stem, in rigid bloom,   120
Grows the salt lavender that lacks perfume;
Here the dwarf sallows creep, the septfoil harsh,
And the soft slimy mallow of the marsh;
Low on the ear the distant billows sound,
And just in view appears their stony bound;
No hedge nor tree conceals the glowing sun,
Birds, save a wat'ry tribe, the district shun,
Nor chirp among the reeds where bitter waters run.
   "Various as beauteous, Nature, is thy face,"
Exclaim'd Orlando: "all that grows has grace;   130
"All are appropriate – bog, and marsh, and fen,
"Are only poor to undiscerning men;
"Here may the nice and curious eye explore
"How Nature's hand adorns the rushy moor;
"Here the rare moss in secret shade is found,
"Here the sweet myrtle of the shaking ground;
"Beauties are these that from the view retire,
"But well repay th'attention they require;
"For these my Laura will her home forsake,
"And all the pleasures they afford partake."   140
   Again the country was enclosed, a wide
And sandy road has banks on either side;
Where, lo! a hollow on the left appear'd,
And there a gipsy-tribe their tent had rear'd;
'Twas open spread, to catch the morning sun,
And they had now their early meal begun,
When two brown boys just left their grassy seat,
The early trav'ller with their pray'rs to greet:
While yet Orlando held his pence in hand,
He saw their sister on her duty stand;   150
Some twelve years old, demure, affected, sly,
Prepared the force of early powers to try;
Sudden a look of languor he descries,
And well-feign'd apprehension in her eyes;

Train'd but yet savage, in her speaking face
He mark'd the features of her vagrant race;
When a light laugh and roguish leer express'd
The vice implanted in her youthful breast:
Forth from the tent her elder brother came,
Who seem'd offended, yet forbore to blame   160
The young designer, but could only trace
The looks of pity in the trav'ller's face:
Within, the father, who from fences nigh
Had brought the fuel for the fire's supply,
Watch'd now the feeble blaze, and stood dejected by:
On ragged rug, just borrow'd from the bed,
And by the hand of coarse indulgence fed,
In dirty patchwork negligently dress'd,
Reclined the wife, an infant at her breast;
In her wild face some touch of grace remain'd,   170
Of vigour palsied and of beauty stain'd;
Her blood-shot eyes on her unheeding mate
Were wrathful turn'd, and seem'd her wants to state,
Cursing his tardy aid – her mother there
With gypsy-state engross'd the only chair;
Solemn and dull her look; with such she stands,
And reads the milk-maid's fortune in her hands,
Tracing the lines of life; assumed through years,
Each feature now the steady falsehood wears;
With hard and savage eye she views the food,   180
And grudging pinches their intruding brood;
Last in the group, the worn-out grandsire sits
Neglected, lost, and living but by fits;
Useless, despised, his worthless labours done,
And half protected by the vicious son,
Who half supports him; he with heavy glance
Views the young ruffians who around him dance;
And, by the sadness in his face, appears
To trace the progress of their future years:
Through what strange course of misery, vice, deceit,   190

145

Must wildly wander each unpractised cheat!
What shame and grief, what punishment and pain,
Sport of fierce passions, must each child sustain –
Ere they like him approach their latter end,
Without a hope, a comfort, or a friend!
  But this Orlando felt not; "Rogues," said he,
"Doubtless they are, but merry rogues they be;
"They wander round the land, and be it true,
"They break the laws – then let the laws pursue
"The wanton idlers; for the life they live,   200
"Acquit I cannot, but I can forgive."
This said, a portion from his purse was thrown,
And every heart seem'd happy like his own.

  He hurried forth, for now the town was nigh –
"The happiest man of mortal men am I."
Thou art! but change in every state is near,
(So while the wretched hope, the blest may fear);
"Say, where is Laura?" – "That her words must show,"
A lass replied; "read this, and thou shalt know!"
  "What, gone!" – her friend insisted – forced to go: –   210
"Is vex'd, was teased, could not refuse her! – No?"
"But you can follow:" "Yes:" "The miles are few,
"The way is pleasant; will you come? – Adieu!
"Thy Laura!" "No! I feel I must resign
"The pleasing hope, thou hadst been here, if mine:
"A lady was it? – Was no brother there?
"But why should I afflict me if there were?"
"The way is pleasant:" "What to me the way?
"I cannot reach her till the close of day.
"My dumb companion! is it thus we speed?   220
"Not I from grief nor thou from toil art freed;
"Still art thou doom'd to travel and to pine,
"For my vexation – What a fate is mine!
  "Gone to a friend, she tells me; I commend
"Her purpose; means she to a female friend?
"By Heaven, I wish she suffer'd half the pain

"Of hope protracted through the day in vain:
"Shall I persist to see th'ungrateful maid?
"Yes, I will see her, slight her, and upbraid:
"What! in the very hour? She knew the time,   230
"And doubtless chose it to increase her crime."
    Forth rode Orlando by a river's side,
Inland and winding, smooth, and full and wide,
That roll'd majestic on, in one soft-flowing tide;
The bottom gravel, flow'ry were the banks,
Tall willows, waving in their broken ranks;
The road, now near, now distant, winding led
By lovely meadows which the waters fed;
He pass'd the way-side inn, the village spire,
Nor stopp'd to gaze, to question, or admire;   240
On either side the rural mansions stood,
With hedge-row trees, and hills high-crown'd with wood,
And many a devious stream that reach'd the nobler flood.
    "I hate these scenes," Orlando angry cried,
"And these proud farmers! yes, I hate their pride:
"See! that sleek fellow, how he strides along,
"Strong as an ox, and ignorant as strong;
"Can yon close crops a single eye detain
"But his who counts the profits of the grain?
"And these vile beans with deleterious smell,   250
"Where is their beauty? can a mortal tell?
"These deep fat meadows I detest; it shocks
"One's feelings there to see the grazing ox; –
"For slaughter fatted, as a lady's smile
"Rejoices man, and means his death the while.
"Lo! now the sons of labour! every day
"Employ'd in toil, and vex'd in every way;
"Theirs is but mirth assumed, and they conceal,
"In their affected joys, the ills they feel:
"I hate these long green lanes; there's nothing seen   260
"In this vile country but eternal green;
"Woods! waters! meadows! Will they never end?

147

"'Tis a vile prospect: – Gone to see a friend!" –
　Still on he rode! a mansion fair and tall
Rose on his view – the pride of Loddon-Hall:
Spread o'er the park he saw the grazing steer,
The full-fed steed, the herds of bounding deer:
On a clear stream the vivid sunbeams play'd,
Through noble elms, and on the surface made
That moving picture, checker'd light and shade;　　　　270
Th'attended children, there indulged to stray,
Enjoy'd and gave new beauty to the day;
Whose happy parents from their room were seen
Pleased with the sportive idlers on the green.
　"Well!" said Orlando, "and for one so bless'd,
"A thousand reasoning wretches are distress'd;
"Nay, these so seeming glad, are grieving like the rest:
"Man is a cheat – and all but strive to hide
"Their inward misery by their outward pride.
"What do yon lofty gates and walls contain,　　　　280
"But fruitless means to soothe unconquer'd pain?
"The parents read each infant daughter's smile,
"Form'd to seduce, encouraged to beguile;
"They view the boys unconscious of their fate,
"Sure to be tempted, sure to take the bait;
"These will be Lauras, sad Orlandos these –
"There's guilt and grief in all one hears and sees."
　Our trav'ller, lab'ring up a hill, look'd down
Upon a lively, busy, pleasant town;
All he beheld were there alert, alive,　　　　290
The busiest bees that ever stock'd a hive:
A pair were married, and the bells aloud
Proclaim'd their joy, and joyful seem'd the crowd;
And now proceeding on his way, he spied,
Bound by strong ties, the bridegroom and the bride:
Each by some friends attended, near they drew,
And spleen beheld them with prophetic view.
　"Married! nay, mad!" Orlando cried in scorn;

"Another wretch on this unlucky morn:
"What are this foolish mirth, these idle joys?   300
"Attempts to stifle doubt and fear by noise:
"To me these robes, expressive of delight,
"Foreshow distress, and only grief excite;
"And for these cheerful friends, will they behold
"Their wailing brood in sickness, want, and cold;
"And his proud look, and her soft languid air
"Will – but I spare you – go, unhappy pair!"
　　And now approaching to the journey's end,
His anger fails, his thoughts to kindness tend,
He less offended feels, and rather fears t'offend: 310
Now gently rising, hope contends with doubt,
And casts a sunshine on the views without;
And still reviving joy and lingering gloom
Alternate empire o'er his soul assume;
Till, long perplex'd, he now began to find
The softer thoughts engross the settling mind:
He saw the mansion, and should quickly see
His Laura's self – and angry could he be?
No! the resentment melted all away –
"For this my grief a single smile will pay,"   320
Our trav'ller cried; – "And why should it offend,
"That one so good should have a pressing friend?
"Grieve not, my heart! to find a favourite guest
"Thy pride and boast – ye selfish sorrows, rest;
"She will be kind, and I again be blest."
　　While gentler passions thus his bosom sway'd,
He reach'd the mansion, and he saw the maid;
"My Laura!" – "My Orlando! – this is kind;
"In truth I came persuaded, not inclined:
"Our friends' amusement let us now pursue,   330
"And I to-morrow will return with you."
　　Like man entranced, the happy lover stood –
"As Laura wills, for she is kind and good;
"Ever the truest, gentlest, fairest, best –

149

"As Laura wills, I see her and am blest."
  Home went the lovers through that busy place,
By Loddon-Hall, the country's pride and grace;
By the rich meadows where the oxen fed,
Through the green vale that form'd the river's bed;
And by unnumber'd cottages and farms,   340
That have for musing minds unnumber'd charms;
And how affected by the view of these
Was then Orlando – did they pain or please?
  Nor pain nor pleasure could they yield – and why?
The mind was fill'd, was happy, and the eye
Roved o'er the fleeting views, that but appear'd to die.
  Alone Orlando on the morrow paced
The well-known road; the gypsy-tent he traced;
The dam high-raised, the reedy dikes between,
The scatter'd hovels on the barren green,   350
The burning sand, the fields of thin-set rye,
Mock'd by the useless Flora, blooming by;
And last the heath with all its various bloom,
And the close lanes that led the trav'ller home.
  Then could these scenes the former joys renew?
Or was there now dejection in the view? –
Nor one or other would they yield – and why?
The mind was absent, and the vacant eye
Wander'd o'er viewless scenes, that but appear'd to die.

Tales of the Hall

Adventures of Richard

[Having had little previous contact with him, Richard is visiting
his elder half-brother at the latter's home.]

Eight days had past; the Brothers now could meet
With ease, and take the customary seat.
"These," said the host, for he perceived where stray'd
His brother's eye, and what he now survey'd;
"These are the costly trifles that we buy,
"Urged by the strong demands of vanity,
"The thirst and hunger of a mind diseased,
"That must with purchased flattery be appeased;
"But yet, 'tis true, the things that you behold
"Serve to amuse us as we're getting old: 10
"These pictures, as I heard our artists say,
"Are genuine all, and I believe they may;
"They cost the genuine sums, and I should grieve
"If, being willing, I could not believe.
"And there is music; when the ladies come,
"With their keen looks they scrutinize the room
"To see what pleases, and I must expect
"To yield them pleasure, or to find neglect:
"For, as attractions from our person fly,
"Our purses, Richard, must the want supply;   20
"Yet would it vex me could the triflers know
"That they can shut out comfort or bestow.

"But see this room: here, Richard, you will find
"Books for all palates, food for every mind;
"This readers term the ever-new delight,
"And so it is, if minds have appetite:
"Mine once was craving; great my joy, indeed,

151

"Had I possess'd such food when I could feed;
"When at the call of every new-born wish
"I could have keenly relish'd every dish –   30
"Now, Richard, now, I stalk around and look
"Upon the dress and title of a book,
"Try half a page, and then can taste no more,
"But the dull volume to its place restore;
"Begin a second slowly to peruse,
"Then cast it by, and look about for news;
"The news itself grows dull in long debates, –
"I skip, and see what the conclusion states;
"And many a speech, with zeal and study made
"Cold and resisting spirits to persuade,   40
"Is lost on mine; alone, we cease to feel
"What crowds admire, and wonder at their zeal.

"But how the day? No fairer will it be?
"Walk you? Alas! 'tis requisite for me –
"Nay, let me not prescribe – my friends and guests are free."
                              *
It was a fair and mild autumnal sky,
And earth's ripe treasures met th'admiring eye,
As a rich beauty, when her bloom is lost,
Appears with more magnificence and cost:
The wet and heavy grass, where feet had stray'd,   50
Not yet erect, the wanderer's way betray'd;
Showers of the night had swell'd the deep'ning rill,
The morning breeze had urged the quick'ning mill;
Assembled rooks had wing'd their sea-ward flight,
By the same passage to return at night,
While proudly o'er them hung the steady kite,
Then turn'd him back, and left the noisy throng,
Nor deign'd to know them as he sail'd along.

Long yellow leaves, from oziers, strew'd around,
Choked the small stream, and hush'd the feeble sound;   60

While the dead foliage dropt from loftier trees
Our squire beheld not with his wonted ease,
But to his own reflections made reply,
And said aloud, "Yes! doubtless we must die."

"We must;" said Richard, "and we would not live
"To feel what dotage and decay will give;
"But we yet taste whatever we behold,
"The morn is lovely, though the air is cold:
"There is delicious quiet in this scene,
"At once so rich, so varied, so serene;   70
"Sounds too delight us, – each discordant tone
"Thus mingled please, that fail to please alone;
"This hollow wind, this rustling of the brook,
"The farm-yard noise, the woodman at yon oak –
"See, the axe falls! – now listen to the stroke!
"That gun itself, that murders all this peace,
"Adds to the charm, because it soon must cease."

"No doubt," said George, "the country has its charms!
"My farm behold! the model for all farms!
"Look at that land – you find there not a weed,   80
"We grub the roots, and suffer none to seed.
"To land like this no botanist will come,
"To seek the precious ware he hides at home;
"Pressing the leaves and flowers with effort nice,
"As if they came from herbs in Paradise;
"Let them their favourites with my neighbours see,
"They have no – what? – no *habitat* with me.

"Now see my flock, and hear its glory; – none
"Have that vast body and that slender bone;
"They are the village boast, the dealer's theme,   90
"Fleece of such staple! flesh in such esteem!"

153

"Brother," said Richard, "do I hear aright?
"Does the land truly give so much delight?"

"So says my bailiff: sometimes I have tried
"To catch the joy, but nature has denied;
"It will not be – the mind has had a store
"Laid up for life, and will admit no more:
"Worn out in trials, and about to die,
"In vain to these we for amusement fly;
"We farm, we garden, we our poor employ,   100
"And much command, though little we enjoy;
"Or, if ambitious, we employ our pen,
"We plant a desert, or we drain a fen;
"And – here, behold my medal! – this will show
"What men may merit when they nothing know."

"Yet reason here," said Richard, "joins with pride: –"
"I did not ask th'alliance," George replied –
"I grant it true, such trifle may induce
"A dull, proud man to wake and be of use;
"And there are purer pleasures, that a mind   110
"Calm and uninjured may in villas find;
"But where th'affections have been deeply tried,
"With other food that mind must be supplied:
"'Tis not in trees or medals to impart
"The powerful medicine for an aching heart;
"The agitation dies, but there is still
"The backward spirit, the resisting will.
"Man takes his body to a country seat,
"But minds, dear Richard, have their own retreat;
"Oft when the feet are pacing o'er the green   120
"The mind is gone where never grass was seen,
"And never thinks of hill, or vale, or plain,
"Till want of rest creates a sense of pain,
"That calls that wandering mind, and brings it home again.
"No more of farms: but here I boast of minds

"That make a friend the richer when he finds;
"These shalt thou see; – but, Richard, be it known,
"Who thinks to see must in his turn be shown: –
"But now farewell! to thee will I resign
"Woods, walks, and valleys! take them till we dine."   130
*
The Brothers dined, and with that plenteous fare
That seldom fails to dissipate our care,
At least the lighter kind; and oft prevails
When reason, duty, nay, when kindness fails.
Yet food and wine, and all that mortals bless,
Lead them to think of peril and distress;
Cold, hunger, danger, solitude, and pain,
That men in life's adventurous ways sustain.

"Thou hast sail'd far, dear brother," said the 'squire –
"Permit me of these unknown lands t'inquire,   140
"Lands never till'd, where thou hast wondering been,
"And all the marvels thou hast heard and seen:
"Do tell me something of the miseries felt
"In climes where travellers freeze, and where they melt;
"And be not nice, – we know 'tis not in men,
"Who travel far, to hold a steady pen:
"Some will, 'tis true, a bolder freedom take,
"And keep our wonder always wide awake;
"We know of those whose dangers far exceed
"Our frail belief, that trembles as we read;   150
"Such as in deserts burn, and thirst, and die,
"Save a last gasp that they recover by:
"Then, too, their hazard from a tyrant's arms,
"A tiger's fury, or a lady's charms;
"Beside th'accumulated evils borne
"From the bold outset to the safe return.
"These men abuse; but thou hast fair pretence
"To modest dealing, and to mild good sense;
"Then let me hear thy struggles and escapes

155

"In the far lands of crocodiles and apes: 160
"Say, hast thou, Bruce-like, knelt upon the bed
"Where the young Nile uplifts his branchy head?
"Or been partaker of th'unhallowed feast,
"Where beast-like man devours his fellow beast,
"And churn'd the bleeding life? while each great dame
"And sovereign beauty bade adieu to shame?
"Or did the storm, that thy wreck'd pinnace bore,
"Impel thee gasping on some unknown shore;
"Where, when thy beard and nails were savage grown,
"Some swarthy princess took thee for her own, 170
"Some danger-dreading Yarico, who, kind,
"Sent thee away, and, prudent, staid behind?

"Come – I am ready wonders to receive,
"Prone to assent, and willing to believe."

Richard replied: "It must be known to you,
"That tales improbable may yet be true;
"And yet it is a foolish thing to tell
"A tale that shall be judged improbable;
"While some impossibilities appear
"So like the truth, that we assenting hear: 180
"Yet, with your leave, I venture to relate
"A chance-affair, and fact alone will state;
"Though, I confess, it may suspicion breed,
"And you may cry, 'improbable, indeed!'
*
"When first I tried the sea, I took a trip,
"But duty none, in a relation's ship;
"Thus, unengaged, I felt my spirits light,
"Kept care at distance, and put fear to flight;
"Oft this same spirit in my friends prevail'd,
"Buoyant in dangers, rising when assail'd; 190
"When, as the gale at evening died away,
"And die it will with the retiring day,

156

"Impatient then, and sick of very ease,
"We loudly whistled for the slumbering breeze.

"One eve it came; and, frantic in my joy,
"I rose and danced, as idle as a boy:
"The cabin-lights were down, that we might learn
"A trifling something from the ship astern;
"The stiffening gale bore up the growing wave,
"And wilder motion to my madness gave: 200
"Oft have I since, when thoughtful and at rest,
"Believed some maddening power my mind possess'd;
"For, in an instant, as the stern sank low,
"(How moved I knew not – What can madness know?)
"Chance that direction to my motion gave,
"And plunged me headlong in the roaring wave:
"Swift flew the parting ship, – the fainter light
"Withdrew, – or horror took them from my sight.

"All was confused above, beneath, around;
"All sounds of terror; no distinguish'd sound   210
"Could reach me, now on sweeping surges tost,
"And then between the rising billows lost;
"An undefined sensation stopp'd my breath;
"Disorder'd views and threat'ning signs of death
"Met in one moment, and a terror gave –
"I cannot paint it – to the moving grave.
"My thoughts were all distressing, hurried, mix'd,
"On all things fixing, not a moment fix'd:
"Vague thoughts of instant danger brought their pain,
"New hopes of safety banish'd them again;   220
"Then the swoln billow all these hopes destroy'd,
"And left me sinking in the mighty void:
"Weaker I grew, and grew the more dismay'd,
"Of aid all hopeless, yet in search of aid;
"Struggling awhile upon the wave to keep,
"Then, languid, sinking in the yawning deep:

157

"So tost, so lost, so sinking in despair,
"I pray'd in heart an indirected prayer,
"And then once more I gave my eyes to view
"The ship now lost, and bade the light adieu!   230
"From my chill'd frame th'enfeebled spirit fled,
"Rose the tall billows round my deep'ning bed,
"Cold seized my heart, thought ceased, and I was dead.

"Brother, I have not, – man has not the power
"To paint the horrors of that life-long hour;
"Hour! – but of time I knew not – when I found
"Hope, youth, life, love, and all they promised, drown'd;
"When all so indistinct, so undefined,
"So dark and dreadful, overcame the mind;
"When such confusion on the spirit dwelt,   240
"That, feeling much, it knew not what it felt.

"Can I, my brother – ought I to forget
"That night of terror? No! it threatens yet.
"Shall I days, months – nay, years, indeed, neglect,
"Who then could feel what moments must effect
"Were aught effected? who, in that wild storm,
"Found there was nothing I could well perform;
"For what to us are moments, what are hours,
"If lost our judgment, and confused our powers?

"Oft in the times when passion strives to reign,   250
"When duty feebly holds the slacken'd chain,
"When reason slumbers, then remembrance draws
"This view of death, and folly makes a pause –
"The view o'ercomes the vice, the fear the frenzy awes.

"I know there wants not this to make it true,
"What danger bids be done, in safety do;
"Yet such escapes may make our purpose sure,
"Who slights such warning may be too secure."

"But the escape!" – "Whate'er they judged might save
"Their sinking friend they cast upon the wave;   260
"Something of these my heaven-directed arm
"Unconscious seized, and held as by a charm:
"The crew astern beheld me as I swam,
"And I am saved – O! let me say I am."

                    *

"Brother," said George, "I have neglected long
"To think of all thy perils: – it was wrong;
"But do forgive me; for I could not be
"Than of myself more negligent of thee.
"Now tell me, Richard, from the boyish years
"Of thy young mind, that now so rich appears,   270
"How was it stored? 'twas told me, thou wert wild,
"A truant urchin, – a neglected child.
"I heard of this escape, and sat supine
"Amid the danger that exceeded thine;
"Thou couldst but die – the waves could but infold
"Thy warm gay heart, and make that bosom cold –
"While I – but no! Proceed, and give me truth;
"How past the years of thy unguided youth?
"Thy father left thee to the care of one
"Who could not teach, could ill support a son;   280
"Yet time and trouble feeble minds have stay'd,
"And fit for long-neglected duties made:
"I see thee struggling in the world, as late
"Within the waves, and with an equal fate,
"By Heaven preserved – but tell me, whence and how
"Thy gleaning came? – a dexterous gleaner thou!"

"Left by that father, who was known to few,
"And to that mother, who has not her due
"Of honest fame," said Richard, "our retreat
"Was a small cottage, for our station meet,   290
"On Barford Downs: that mother, fond and poor,
"There taught some truths, and bade me seek for more,

"Such as our village-school and books a few
"Supplied; but such I cared not to pursue;
"I sought the town, and to the ocean gave
"My mind and thoughts, as restless as the wave:
"Where crowds assembled, I was sure to run,
"Hear what was said, and mused on what was done;
"Attentive listening in the moving scene,
"And often wondering what the men could mean.   300

"When ships at sea made signals of their need,
"I watch'd on shore the sailors, and their speed:
"Mix'd in their act, nor rested till I knew
"Why they were call'd, and what they were to do.

"Whatever business in the port was done,
"I, without call, was with the busy one;
"Not daring question, but with open ear
"And greedy spirit, ever bent to hear.

"To me the wives of seamen loved to tell
"What storms endanger'd men esteem'd so well;   310
"What wond'rous things in foreign parts they saw,
"Lands without bounds, and people without law.

"No ships were wreck'd upon that fatal beach,
"But I could give the luckless tale of each;
"Eager I look'd, till I beheld a face
"Of one disposed to paint their dismal case;
"Who gave the sad survivors' doleful tale,
"From the first brushing of the mighty gale
"Until they struck; and, suffering in their fate,
"I long'd the more they should its horrors state;   320
"While some, the fond of pity, would enjoy
"The earnest sorrows of the feeling boy.
"I sought the men return'd from regions cold,
"The frozen straits, where icy mountains roll'd;

160

"Some I could win to tell me serious tales
"Of boats uplifted by enormous whales,
"Or, when harpoon'd, how swiftly through the sea
"The wounded monsters with the cordage flee;
"Yet some uneasy thoughts assail'd me then,
"The monsters warr'd not with, nor wounded men: 330
"The smaller fry we take, with scales and fins,
"Who gasp and die – this adds not to our sins;
"But so much blood! warm life, and frames so large
"To strike, to murder – seem'd an heavy charge.

"They told of days, where many goes to one –
"Such days as ours; and how a larger sun,
"Red, but not flaming, roll'd, with motion slow,
"On the world's edge, and never dropt below.

"There were fond girls, who took me to their side
"To tell the story how their lovers died;   340
"They praised my tender heart, and bade me prove
"Both kind and constant when I came to love.
"In fact, I lived for many an idle year
"In fond pursuit of agitations dear;
"For ever seeking, ever pleased to find,
"The food I loved, I thought not of its kind;
"It gave affliction while it brought delight,
"And joy and anguish could at once excite.

"One gusty day, now stormy and now still,
"I stood apart upon the western hill,   350
"And saw a race at sea: a gun was heard,
"And two contending boats in sail appear'd:
"Equal awhile; then one was left behind,
"And for a moment had her chance resign'd,
"When, in that moment, up a sail they drew –
"Not used before – their rivals to pursue.
"Strong was the gale! in hurry now there came

161

"Men from the town, their thoughts, their fears the same;
"And women too! affrighted maids and wives,
"All deeply feeling for their sailors' lives. 360

"The strife continued; in a glass we saw
"The desperate efforts, and we stood in awe,
"When the last boat shot suddenly before,
"Then fill'd, and sank – and could be seen no more!

"Then were those piercing shrieks, that frantic flight,
"All hurried! all in tumult and affright!
"A gathering crowd from different streets drew near,
"All ask, all answer – none attend, none hear!

"One boat is safe; and see! she backs her sail
"To save the sinking – Will her care avail? 370

"O! how impatient on the sands we tread,
"And the winds roaring, and the women led,
"As up and down they pace with frantic air,
"And scorn a comforter, and will despair;
"They know not who in either boat is gone,
"But think the father, husband, lover, one.

"And who is she apart? She dares not come
"To join the crowd, yet cannot rest at home:
"With what strong interest looks she at the waves,
"Meeting and clashing o'er the seamen's graves: 380
"'Tis a poor girl betroth'd – a few hours more,
"And *he* will lie a corpse upon the shore.

"Strange, that a boy could love these scenes, and cry
"In very pity – but that boy was I.
"With pain my mother would my tales receive,
"And say, 'my Richard, do not learn to grieve.'

"One wretched hour had past before we knew
"Whom they had saved! Alas! they were but two,
"An orphan'd lad and widow'd man – no more!
"And they unnoticed stood upon the shore,   390
"With scarce a friend to greet them – widows view'd
"This man and boy, and then their cries renew'd: –
"'Twas long before the signs of wo gave place
"To joy again; grief sat on every face.

"Sure of my mother's kindness, and the joy
"She felt in meeting her rebellious boy,
"I at my pleasure our new seat forsook,
"And, undirected, these excursions took:
"I often rambled to the noisy quay,
"Strange sounds to hear, and business strange to me;   400
"Seamen and carmen, and I know not who,
"A lewd, amphibious, rude, contentious crew –
"Confused as bees appear about their hive,
"Yet all alert to keep their work alive.

"Here, unobserved as weed upon the wave,
"My whole attention to the scene I gave;
"I saw their tasks, their toil, their care, their skill,
"Led by their own and by a master-will;
"And though contending, toiling, tugging on,
"The purposed business of the day was done.   410

"The open shops of craftsmen caught my eye,
"And there my questions met the kind reply:
"Men, when alone, will teach; but, in a crowd,
"The child is silent, or the man is proud;
"But, by themselves, there is attention paid
"To a mild boy, so forward, yet afraid.

"I made me interest at the inn's fire-side,
"Amid the scenes to bolder boys denied;

163

"For I had patrons there, and I was one,
"They judged, who noticed nothing that was done.   420
"'A quiet lad!' would my protector say;
"'To him, now, this is better than his play:
"'Boys are as men; some active, shrewd, and keen,
"'They look about if aught is to be seen;
"'And some, like Richard here, have not a mind
"'That takes a notice – but the lad is kind.'

"I loved in summer on the heath to walk,
"And seek the shepherd – shepherds love to talk:
"His superstition was of ranker kind,
"And he with tales of wonder stored my mind;   430
"Wonders that he in many a lonely eve
"Had seen himself, and therefore must believe.
"His boy, his Joe, he said, from duty ran,
"Took to the sea, and grew a fearless man:
"'On yonder knoll – the sheep were in the fold –
"'His spirit past me, shivering-like and cold!
"'I felt a fluttering, but I knew not how,
"'And heard him utter, like a whisper, 'now!'
"'Soon came a letter from a friend – to tell
"'That he had fallen, and the time he fell.'   440

"Even to the smugglers' hut the rocks between,
"I have, adventurous in my wandering, been:
"Poor, pious Martha served the lawless tribe,
"And could their merits and their faults describe;
"Adding her thoughts; 'I talk, my child, to you,
"'Who little think of what such wretches do.'

"I loved to walk where none had walk'd before,
"About the rocks that ran along the shore;
"Or far beyond the sight of men to stray,
"And take my pleasure when I lost my way;   450
"For then 'twas mine to trace the hilly heath,

164

"And all the mossy moor that lies beneath:
"Here had I favourite stations, where I stood
"And heard the murmurs of the ocean-flood,
"With not a sound beside, except when flew
"Aloft the lapwing, or the gray curlew,
"Who with wild notes my fancied power defied,
"And mock'd the dreams of solitary pride.

"I loved to stop at every creek and bay
"Made by the river in its winding way,   460
"And call to memory – not by marks they bare,
"But by the thoughts that were created there.

"Pleasant it was to view the sea-gulls strive
"Against the storm, or in the ocean dive,
"With eager scream, or when they dropping gave
"Their closing wings to sail upon the wave:
"Then as the winds and waters raged around,
"And breaking billows mix'd their deafening sound,
"They on the rolling deep securely hung,
"And calmly rode the restless waves among.   470
"Nor pleased it less around me to behold,
"Far up the beach, the yesty sea-foam roll'd;
"Or from the shore upborn, to see on high,
"Its frothy flakes in wild confusion fly:
"While the salt spray that clashing billows form,
"Gave to the taste a feeling of the storm.

"Thus, with my favourite views, for many an hour
"Have I indulged the dreams of princely power;
"When the mind, wearied by excursions bold,
"The fancy jaded, and the bosom cold,   480
"Or when those wants, that will on kings intrude,
"Or evening-fears, broke in on solitude;
"When I no more my fancy could employ,

165

"I left in haste what I could not enjoy,
"And was my gentle mother's welcome boy.

"But now thy walk, – this soft autumnal gloom
"Bids no delay – at night I will resume
"My subject, showing, not how I improved
"In my strange school, but what the things I loved,
"My first-born friendships, ties by forms uncheck'd,   490
"And all that boys acquire whom men neglect."

Notes

Where this has seemed desirable I have used Crabbe's own notes, which are indicated thus: (C).

The Village

Page 17, line 16 *Tityrus* The fortunate shepherd of Virgil's first eclogue. Line 27 *Duck* Stephen Duck (1705-56). An agricultural labourer from Wiltshire who, profiting from the patronage of Queen Caroline, acquired a short-lived reputation as a poet.

The Parish Register

Page 36, line 323 *Joseph* A long buttoned cloak with a small cape.

The Borough

Page 41, line 41 *Sampire* [Samphire]. The jointed glasswort, *Salicornia*, is here meant, not the true sampire, the *Crithmum maritimum* (C). Line 52 *Hoys....snows* All are varieties of sailing vessel.
Page 43, line 130 *Tenters* Hooked spikes. Line 134 *"Like a tall bully....lies."* Borrowed (with the substitution of 'its' for 'the') from Pope's *Moral Essays*, Epistle III.
Page 44, line 147 *Crag* A shelly sand found in Norfolk, Suffolk and Essex. Line 150 *Gale* The bog-myrtle.
Page 51, line 84 *....and from that its name;* Jelly-fish or Medusae are also known as sea-nettles.
Page 52, line 140 *Pam* The card-game.

Page 115, line 40   *saints*   This appellation is here used not ironically nor with malignity; but it is taken merely to designate a morosely devout people, with peculiar austerity of manners (C).

Page 129, line 29   *frustums*   Fragments.

Page 142, line 67   *black-legs*   Race-course swindlers.

Tales of the Hall

Page 156, line 161   *Bruce-like*   James Bruce (1730-94), explorer and antiquary.